BLUEPRINTS
FOR WORSHIP

BLUEPRINTS FOR WORSHIP

A User's Guide for United Methodist Congregations

Andy Langford

Abingdon Press
Nashville

Blueprints for Worship: A User's Guide for United Methodist Congregations

Copyright © 1993 by Abingdon Press

This book is printed on recycled, acid-free paper.

Library of Congress Cataloging-in-Publication Data

Langford, Andy.
  Blueprints for worship: a user's guide for United Methodist congregations/Andy Langford.
      p. cm.
  Includes bibliographical references and index.
  ISBN 0-687-03312-8 (alk. paper)
    1. United Methodist Church (U.S.)—Liturgy. 2. Methodist Church—Liturgy. 3. Church year. I. Title.
  BX8382.2.Z5L35   1993
  264'.076—dc20   92-41992

Versions of several of the worksheets and comments found in this volume have appeared previously in other publications of The Section on Worship of The General Board of Discipleship. These include: "Planning for Worship," written with Hoyt Hickman, Diana Sanchez, and Michael Williams; "Preparing to Preach," written with Michael Williams; "Congregational Singing," which first appeared as "Becoming a Singing Congregation" in *The Hymns of The United Methodist Hymnal*, written with Diana Sanchez; "Wedding Worksheet," written by M. Lawrence Snot; and "Funeral Worksheet."

All quotations regarding worship services and rubrics are taken from *The United Methodist Book of Worship*. Copyright 1992 by The United Methodist Publishing House. Used by permission.

Scripture quotations, unless otherwise indicated, are from the New Revised Standard Version of the Bible, copyright 1989 by the Division of Christian Education of the National Council of Churches of Christ in the USA. Used by permission.

93 94 95 96 97 98 99 00 01 02 — 10 9 8 7 6 5 4 3 2 1

MANUFACTURED IN THE UNITED STATES OF AMERICA

This book is dedicated
to all who nurtured me in worship:
my grandmothers,
Ann Lambeth Daniel and Louie Mae Hughes Langford;
my parents,
Tom and Marie Langford;
and it is written for my daughters,
Ann Green and Sarah Langford,
and for all children who will discover God through worship.

CONTENTS

CONTENTS

PREFACE

While I was in the midst of writing this book, my brother Jay, a builder, was constructing his new home in the mountains of North Carolina. My other two brothers, Tim and Hugh, who are also carpenters, came to help him. Then, with some reluctance, Jay invited me one weekend to carry lumber and hammer some nails. Standing (very nervously) thirty feet off the ground on a two-by-four piece of pine lumber, I learned anew the complex and detailed task of putting together a new building. Each piece of material needed to go in the right place, at the right time, and with exactly the correct measurements. If one board in one rafter was one quarter of an inch off, the whole roof, and thus the whole building, could later develop significant problems. After one weekend, I realized again that I am not a builder of new homes.

Worship, likewise, is just as complex a task. Putting together scripture lessons, hymns, prayers, visuals, and many other parts of worship for a specific congregation is equally difficult. Designers and leaders of worship also need to know what they desire to accomplish, have in hand the correct tools, use the right materials, and put all of the parts together with expertise and artistry. This book provides you—an architect and builder of worship—some of the tools and materials you need to create vital worship week after week in your local congregation.

This resource rests on the two foundational worship documents of our United Methodist Church: *The United Methodist Hymnal* and *The United Methodist Book of Worship*. These two books include the basic material that every United Methodist planner and leader of worship needs to design and to lead congregational worship. This resource will enhance your use of these books, whether or not you know these books well. It does not demand that you must plan in only one way or use one particular resource; it does tell you how to use with quality a vast array of services.

This work was not done alone. Profound appreciation goes to the members of The Hymnal Revision Committee and The United Methodist Book of Worship Committee, voting members of The Section on Worship of The General Board of Discipleship from 1985 to 1992, the professors of worship, music, and preaching throughout our denomination with whom I have worked, and the countless pastors, musicians, and worship committee members in local congregations, all of whom have contributed to worship renewal in our Church. I also thank Ezra Earl Jones and Alan Waltz, my supervisors at the General Board of Discipleship, for their patience and guidance. The transformation of worship in our denomination over the past twenty years is directly attributable to the vision, energy, and work of all these people.

Especially, I offer thanks to the staff of the Section on Worship, with whom I have been blessed to work. Their love of God, their loyalty to our denomination, and their passion for grace-filled worship have changed many lives. While some of their names are known to many United Methodists, others in anonymity have also shaped our worship. These friends are:

Barbara Bate, who listens and preaches well;
David Bone, one of the world's best accompanists;
Verlia Burns, who taught us all how to use computers;
Nylea Butler-Moore, a steady and stable colleague and musician;
Tim Edmonds, an enthusiastic musician;
Hoyt Hickman, my worship mentor and dean of United Methodist liturgists;
Joane Jordan, who assisted in all my work and held us all together;
Diana Sanchez, a passionate advocate for congregational song; and
Michael Williams, a preacher of holy tales and a friend.

I offer this work to all who create and guide worship in The United Methodist Church. May this book strengthen your worship and empower your congregation's ministry and mission, and may God's grace be with you.

Andy Langford
Nashville
Day of Pentecost, 1992

PART ONE:

BUILDING BLOCKS OF UNITED METHODIST WORSHIP

INTRODUCTION

I was glad when they said to me,
"Let us go to the house of the LORD!"
                    (PS. 122:1)

When Christians gather to hear the Word, to baptize, to eat and drink, to pray, and to become the living body of Christ, the Church is at worship. Throughout the history of the Church universal, and particularly within our own Wesleyan tradition, worship affords congregations the opportunity to praise God, and it has been the way through which the prevenient, justifying, and sanctifying grace of God saves. In worship, your congregation remembers who it is, rehearses its story, and becomes a new creation.

More people, expectant and eager, attend your congregation's worship than attend any other activity of your local congregation. A good Sunday morning service, a reverent funeral, a celebrative wedding, or a joyous hymn festival can provide an occasion in which God and your people become one. Worship that is faithful to Scripture, obedient to our tradition, reflective of sound theology, and sensitive to human experience can change lives, prompt the renewal of your congregation, and maybe even save our entire denomination.

Worship is the heart and soul of every ministry of your church. If your worship consists of dry, rigid orders from the past, your church will die. If your worship, however, becomes the focus of life of every member in your congregation, your church will live. Many of the difficulties in congregations today occur because leaders of worship have not paid serious attention to how congregations encounter Scripture, share the holy meal, baptize, pray, and share Christian fellowship. Yet, it is precisely in worship that God offers God's own self to your congregation and forms your people into new creations.

This resource provides practical assistance for you—the pastors, musicians, and others who plan and lead worship in local congregations. Based on *The United Methodist Hymnal* and *The United Methodist Book of*

11

Worship, it enables you to create, design, build, and lead effective worship experiences in your local congregation. Planning is the first and most important step in building strong worship. The commentary and worksheets in the book will enable your planning. They will alert you in advance to critical issues and propose many suggestions for a wide variety of worship experiences.

1. FOUR FOUNDATION STONES

Peter said to them, "Repent, and be baptized every one of you in the name of Jesus Christ so that your sins may be forgiven; and you will receive the gift of the Holy Spirit. . . ." So those who welcomed his message were baptized, and that day about three thousand persons were added. They devoted themselves to the apostles' teaching and fellowship, to the breaking of bread and the prayers. (ACTS 2:38, 41-42)

In The United Methodist Church today there exists a deep need to return to the foundation stones, the bedrock elements, of worship. Upon these rocks rest all of our worship together. We cannot plan worship without understanding these foundations. During the past twenty years, worship has undergone many changes. In the midst of all these changes, however, the essential elements of worship have been less clear for many United Methodists. While fundamental emphases underlie all worship reform, many persons seem uncertain about these foundation stones. Through a rediscovery of our own Wesleyan traditions and an appreciation of ecumenical liturgical advances, United Methodists have rewritten all of our services of worship. The theology and practice of our worship have changed more in the last twenty years than in the previous two hundred years. With *The United Methodist Hymnal* and *The United Methodist Book of Worship*, these basic reforms in worship have become a part of our life together.

The four foundation stones for worship include the **Word of God** read aloud, proclaimed, and heard; the **sacraments of Baptism** and **Holy Communion** rightly taught and practiced; **prayer** offered and received; and **fellowship** in the community by work and sign. Effective congregational worship emphasizes regularly and consistently all four of these essential elements. When your congregation and your people experience the Word of God, the sacraments, prayer, and fellowship in ways that speak to the whole of human life and the community, and then are enabled to respond to God's grace, at that moment God becomes visible and real. Persons are convicted of their sin, recognize that they are children of God, and move toward holy living.

The call to return to these four essential elements of worship is faithful to our Wesleyan tradition. John Wesley declared that God offered, through Jesus Christ and the Holy Spirit, saving grace to every man, woman, and child. The prevenient grace of God convicted people of their sin; justifying grace made them children of the Almighty; sanctifying grace led them to perfection. And Wesley believed that people appropriated such grace through the interaction of the divine and the human: "Upon God's part, his great love and mercy; upon Christ's part, the satisfaction of God's justice, by the offering of his body, and shedding his blood; and upon our part, true and living faith in the merits of Jesus Christ."[1] God's love, Christ's atonement, and human faith by the power of the Holy Spirit issued in conviction, justification, and sanctification. This was the heart of Wesley's message.

Wesley proclaimed salvation through grace and faith. But how were people convicted, justified, and sanctified? How was faith evoked? John and Charles Wesley posed these questions in their hymn "The Bloody Issue Cured":

> How shall a Sinner come to God?
> A Fountain of polluted Blood
> For Years my Plague hath been,
> From Adam the Infection came,
> My Nature is with his the same,
> The same with his my Sin.

The answer the Wesleys provided became the cornerstone of their revival:

> His Body doth the Cure dispense,
> His Garment is the Ordinance
> In which He deigns to' appear;
> The Word, the Prayer, the Broken Bread,
> Virtue from Him doth here proceed,
> And I shall find Him here.[2]

The Word, the Prayer, the Broken Bread, and as Wesley added, Christian fellowship, channeled God's grace to people. John Wesley, living in a society in which holy living meant little, was found by God through worship. David Lowes Watson describes Wesley's view: "Whatever experience of the Holy Spirit might be granted to a person by grace, the means of grace were the necessary structure of that person's spiritual life."[3] The instituted means of grace were, according to Wesley, "the ordinary channels whereby" God might convey to all faithful persons "preventing, justifying, and sanctifying grace."[4] These elements of worship called persons to faithful discipleship.

In summary, Wesley proclaimed that worship, in which God's grace united with individual faith through the liturgical patterns of the church, was the means through which God offered salvation. Wesley held that God ordained these particular signs, words, and actions as the ordinary channels through which grace and faith were joined for salvation: "There is but one scriptural way wherein we receive inward grace—through the outward means which God hath ordained."[5]

Today, United Methodists again emphasize that the Word of God, Baptism, the Lord's Supper, prayer, and fellowship belong to all God's people and call every person to respond with faithful living. By building on these foundation stones, your ministry through worship will make Christian disciples in your congregation.

Worship is the ordinary means by which God is offered to the broken people in your local congregation. The goal of this book is not aesthetically sound or rigidly correct liturgy, but worship that effects a deeper relationship between God, the Church, and all who need God's saving power. Liturgy through Word, sacraments, prayer, and fellowship can create a moral reformation of creation. God's power to convict, justify, and sanctify through worship can help individuals and our Church turn to Jesus Christ, be found by God, and exhibit holy living. As the people of God in worship receive and respond to God's grace, then God will establish the Church as a divine colony that is able to stand against and even overcome the pretensions and illusions of this world.

THE WORD OF GOD

When [Jesus] came to Nazareth, where he had been brought up, he went to the synagogue on the sabbath day, as was his custom. He stood up to read, and the scroll of the prophet Isaiah was given to him. He unrolled the scroll and found the place where it was written:
"The Spirit of the Lord is upon me,
  because he has anointed me
    to bring good news to the poor.
He has sent me to proclaim release
    to the captives
  and recovery of sight to the blind,
  to let the oppressed go free,
to proclaim the year of the Lord's favor." . . .
Then he began to say to them, "Today this scripture has been fulfilled in your hearing." (LUKE 4:16-19, 21)

The Word of God read, proclaimed, and heard is the first foundation stone of worship. John Wesley claimed that he was a man of one book. His own devotional life and his ministry centered on the Bible. Furthermore, Wesley believed that all Christians should read, hear, and meditate on Scripture. Wesley particularly emphasized the Word preached, which, when faithfully heard, became the "chief, ordinary means, whereby God changes both the hearts and lives of sinners."[6]

The Word of God read, proclaimed, and heard is the cornerstone of the renewal of United Methodist worship. The Bible must regain its central role and authority. Every one of the new services of worship in *The United Methodist Hymnal* and *The United Methodist Book of Worship* places the Bible read, proclaimed, and heard at the heart of worship.

Simply reading Scripture, however, is not usually sufficient. Preaching the Word links the Scripture with human life. Worship is incomplete without a sermon, and planning worship without planning preaching is similar to planning a house without designing a floor plan.

Reading and preaching the Word, however, are still not enough. The Word of God, to become flesh, must call forth a response from those who hear. John Wesley, an Arminian (a Christian who emphasized personal responsibility) believed that an individual's responses were integral to salvation. Wesley always asked, "What say you to this?" Or, in contemporary language, "So what?" Preachers in the Wesleyan tradition have historically called for discipleship following a sermon. Prayers, testimonies, hymns, offerings, and a multitude of other responses enable individuals and congregations to answer the call. The arts in the Church—drama, dance, visuals, and the like—also represent vital responses. Many United Methodist congregations have remembered that responses may be unpredictable, spontaneous, and from the heart.

All the new orders of worship in our denomination, as they are found in *The United Methodist Hymnal* and *The United Methodist Book of Worship*, reflect the priority of this first element of worship: reading, proclaiming, and responding to the Word of God. When your congregation in every service of worship hears the Bible read centrally, listens to the Word proclaimed with authority, and is invited to respond to God's call, then your congregation is renewed.

THE SACRAMENTS

While they were eating, Jesus took a loaf of bread, and after blessing it he broke it, gave it to the disciples, and said, "Take, eat; this is my body." Then he took a cup, and after giving thanks he gave it to them, saying, "Drink from it, all of you; for this is my blood of the covenant, which is poured out for many for the forgiveness of sins." (MATT. 26:26-28)

> *And Jesus came and said to them, "All authority in heaven and on earth has been given to me. Go therefore and make disciples of all nations, baptizing them in the name of the Father and of the Son and of the Holy Spirit." (MATT. 28:18-19)*

Baptism and the Lord's Supper are the second foundation stone of worship. Baptized as an infant and confirmed as a child, John Wesley sustained the Baptismal Covenant by the Lord's Supper. He received the holy meal, on average, every four days throughout his life. Wesley said that the sacraments are: "Ordained of Christ to be not only badges or tokens of Christians' profession, but rather they be certain signs of grace, and God's good will toward us, by which he doth work invisibly in us, and doth not only quicken, but also strengthen and confirm our faith in him."[7]

The sacraments are primary to United Methodist worship. Each sacrament offers God's prevenient, justifying, and sanctifying grace, and worshipers are called to respond. Baptism calls persons into Christian discipleship, and the Lord's Supper offers food for the spiritual pilgrimage.

The orders for the sacraments in *The United Methodist Hymnal* and *The United Methodist Book of Worship* are the most ecumenical and yet the most Wesleyan sacramental rites United Methodists have ever possessed. These services, based on the best academic and pastoral advice available, open for our denomination the full power of the Gospel.

Holy Communion, as found in "The Services of Word and Table" in *The United Methodist Hymnal* and *The United Methodist Book of Worship*, declares the fundamental unity between the Word of God and the Lord's Supper. The holy meal is the logical consequence of the Word, and the open invitation to communion is clearly an invitation to grace. Many congregations observe Holy Communion with greater frequency and with such great joy. Many of our congregations are discovering what African American United Methodists have known for so long, that the Lord's Supper is the highlight of worship life.

The Baptismal Covenant, as found in our hymnal and book of worship, provides individuals and congregations the opportunity to renounce the spiritual forces of wickedness, accept the freedom and power God gives, confess Jesus Christ as Savior, commit themselves to the Church, profess the Christian faith, and be saved through water and the Spirit. There is no greater need in our denomination than to recapture the full vitality of our covenant with God through baptism.

Baptism and the Lord's Supper are critical to our worship. When your congregation receives the power that God offers through these sacraments, then your congregation and every member will be strengthened in the pilgrimage toward God.

PRAYER

"Ask, and it will be given you; search, and you will find; knock, and the door will be opened for you. For everyone who asks receives, and everyone who searches finds, and for everyone who knocks, the door will be opened." (MATT. 7:7-8)

Prayer is a primary means through which all worshipers communicate with God, and it is the third foundation stone of worship. John Wesley offered prayer to God every hour on the hour throughout his life as a means of salvation, and he declared: "For thus saith the Lord, 'Ask, and it shall be given to you.' Here, God plainly ordains prayer as the means of receiving whatever grace we want."[8] Because many persons pray only at corporate worship, worship experiences must enable the whole congregation, clergy and laity, to be opened to God through prayer.

In conformity with our Wesleyan tradition, prayer may be of two kinds: formal and free. The historic prayers of the church, as well as those composed by the sensitive souls of our time, are important media by which the Church speaks and listens to the Lord. In addition, spontaneous vocal or silent prayers of persons also communicate. *The United Methodist Book of Worship* encourages your congregation to offer a mixture of printed, formal prayers and flexible, open prayers. Through the new patterns of worship many persons now are given the guidance and freedom to speak and to listen to God through prayer.

Prayer services themselves are also a vital form of corporate worship. From small cells of prayer partners to family prayer time to Wednesday evening prayer services to charismatic prayer and praise services to services of morning, midday, evening, and night prayers, United Methodists are recovering the richness of corporate prayer life. Toward this end, the hymnal and the book of worship include a significant new series of services: Orders of Daily Praise and Prayer. Many United Methodist congregations are approaching prayer not as something to do once a week, but as the way to live.

Furthermore, in both weekly worship and in prayer services, the use of the psalms strengthens our worship. Psalms, the prayer book of God's people, enables our Church to use Scripture as God's prayer with us. As individuals and congregations pray the psalter through word and especially music, whole lives are enriched. The recovery of the psalms in your corporate worship may be the single most significant factor in helping your church again learn how to pray.

The priesthood of all believers is becoming most evident in congregations that reemphasize the third foundation stone of worship: prayer. When your church both speaks and listens to the Lord through prayer, your community becomes Christ at prayer, God's will becomes present, and all are enabled to follow God's pathway.

FELLOWSHIP

All who believed were together and had all things in common. (ACTS 2:44)

Christian conference or fellowship is the fourth foundation stone of worship, and it is the context for all the other means of grace. Christians grow in grace and faith when they gather with one another. John Wesley's own life was lived in Christian community with others, from his early days as a part of Samuel and Susanna's family, to his participation in the Holy Club and his constant participation in classes and bands. The Wesleyan revival became rooted and solid because of the fellowship Wesley created among his followers. When people come together and share their lives with each other, Wesley said, such fellowship can "minister grace—be a means of conveying more grace into their hearts."[9]

United Methodists have always been a people who thrive on Christian fellowship. Worship must exhibit your congregation's love and deepen their relationships with each other. Christian fellowship, the community gathered to encounter the Word of God, to receive the sacraments, and to pray, is "liturgy." By definition liturgy is "the work of the people," and the people together can do the work as one.

At least four elements are essential to strong fellowship in congregational worship. First, our worship pleases God it is when open to all people of all ages, conditions, races, and backgrounds. Our congregations can affirm the diversity of the people gathered yet also minister to all as one body. To do this, your church will reach out especially to persons who have been isolated from the community. Every worship service, for example, that intentionally involves your children or persons with handicapping conditions, not with ministries outside of corporate worship but as an essential part of worship that strengthens all who gather, is a more effective worship service because we are bound together in God's presence and not segregated into convenient cliques.

Second, our worship will enable all who gather together to share their faith together. For example, when a congregation focuses less on worship bulletins, allows persons to look at and speak to each other, encourages common prayer, and enables the sharing of gifts that each person possesses, worship can become more dynamic, spontaneous, and focused on celebrating God's presence.

Third, an emphasis on fellowship will help your congregation be open to receive the rich variety of gifts within your worshiping community. Artists, dancers, musicians, and dramatists each have talents that should be shared and that will strengthen others who receive those gifts. Move beyond good aesthetics and right rubrics that describe only one style or form of art as proper, and offer more variety in your worship. Encourage the multiplicity of gifts resident in your congregation.

Fourth, and a central element of any service of worship, is music and song. The Wesleys opened the music ministry of the Church to all Christians. For two hundred years, singing people have characterized our Church. Over the past several years, United Methodists have rediscovered the richness of our musical heritage. Through congregational song, we affirm our diversity, share our faith, and share in the gifts of the community. Music again belongs to the whole congregation. When people sing, they praise God, respond to God, express their emotions, affirm their faith, and experience community. When your music is alive, your church is alive.

Fellowship, the final foundation stone of worship, is critical as we define who we are as United Methodists. When in our worship we acknowledge our diversity yet affirm our unity, we share our faith, we use our gifts, and we sing, then we fully are a part of God's Kingdom.

The four foundation stones of worship are critical for the future of your congregation and The United Methodist Church. The ministry of the Church through the Word, sacraments, prayer, and fellowship enables God to call our denomination and all our people to discipleship. Even more important, worship also enables our denomination and all who hear to respond to that call. By emphasizing these foundations, the Church will flourish as the body of Christ as the leaders and laity work together to proclaim God's good news.

Praise the Lord!
Praise God in his sanctuary;
  praise him in his mighty firmament!
Praise him for his mighty deeds;
  praise him according to his surpassing greatness!

Praise him with trumpet sound;
  praise him with lute and harp!
Praise him with tambourine and dance;
  praise him with strings and pipe!

Praise him with clanging cymbals;
praise him with loud clashing cymbals!
Let everything that breathes praise the LORD!
Praise the LORD! (Psalm 150)

NOTES

1. John Wesley, *Works VIII* (Grand Rapids: Zondervan, 1958), p. 187.
2. John Wesley and Charles Wesley, *Hymns and Sacred Poems* (London, 1749), pp. 168-69.
3. David Watson, *The Early Methodist Class Meeting* (Nashville: Discipleship Resources, 1985), p. 238.
4. Wesley, *Works VIII*, p. 187.
5. John Telford, *The Letters of John Wesley III* (London: Epworth, 1931), pp. 366-67.
6. John Wesley, *Standard Sermons* (London: Epworth, 1961), p. 493.
7. John Wesley, *The Sunday Service* (London, 1784), pp. 306-312.
8. Nehemiah Curnock, *The Journal of John Welsey II* (London: Epworth, 1939), p. 360.
9. Wesley, *Works VI*, p. 285.
10. *The United Methodist Liturgical Psalter* (Nashville: Abingdon Press, 1989), p. 862.

2. PLANNING FOR WORSHIP

In worship the community of faith celebrates the mighty acts of God and is formed by God's living Word. Yet, good celebration demands planning. At least once a week, and often more frequently, the pastors, musicians, and other worship leaders in your congregation must choose Scripture lessons, prepare sermons, pick hymns, learn music, and make many other decisions.

The following process is one illustration of how to plan for your congregation. You are encouraged to develop your own planning technique. But if you are not satisfied with your own plan, this model is a good starting point.

The first five steps are typically done by the pastor. These steps require a brief, yet intentional, time of looking ahead.

1. Set aside at least half a day to plan according to the seasons of the Christian year. Using a calendar, plan in advance for a whole season of the year at a time, at least eight weeks before the season begins. For example, no later than October 1 plan for the Advent/Christmas/Epiphany cycle; the First Sunday of Advent to the Day of Epiphany. No later than January 1, plan for the Lent/Easter/Pentecost cycle: Ash Wednesday to the Day of Pentecost. And no later than April 1 plan for June, July, and August. Determine which services will be held during that season. Certainly include every Sunday and then add any special services such as a Christmas Eve, Ash Wednesday, or a revival or preaching mission. Review the contents page of *The United Methodist Book of Worship* (4-11) to remind yourself of the variety of services and acts of worship that are possible.

■ Make one copy of the model worksheet at the end of this chapter for every service. If you use a computer, create a template on your hard disk or on a dedicated diskette.

■ Enter the date and day of the service.

■ Create a file folder for each service. The file folder will collect all the resources that you discover as you plan this service of worship. Imaging devices for use with a computer are now too expensive for all but the largest churches, but these devices in the future will make your planning a paperless process as you store resources on electronic media.

2. Choose Scripture lessons and enter them on the worksheet. The preaching pastor typically selects the Bible passages that are at the core of each service of worship.

■ The *Revised Common Lectionary*—a three-year cycle of selected Old Testament, Psalm, Epistle, and New Testament readings (see *UMBOW* 227)—offers one way to choose Scripture. The lectionary was created to make pre-planning simple.

A pastor may choose Scripture based on a theme or themes for the whole season. Or a pastor may decide to use one book of the Bible and work through that book during a particular season. If you choose either of these options, be intentional in covering both the Old Testament and the New Testament over a period of time. Write down the lessons on the worksheet.

■ Read the lessons for each service. If you are using the Revised Common Lectionary, a helpful resource is available: *The Lectionary Bible*. It contains the complete text of the Sunday lessons.

■ Select the primary lesson that will be the cornerstone of the service. The lesson may be from the Old or the New Testament, and it will guide the whole shape of the service. Put a star beside the primary lesson for every service.

3. Choose the sermon focus. The sermon links the Bible with the people and the church. The sermon focus—the basic image, statement, or desired impact that guides the sermon—will give direction to the service. The preacher might ask: How does the Scripture affect me and this congregation? Where does the Scripture challenge or confront? Where does the Scripture comfort? What is missing from the Scripture selected? What responses does the Scripture call forth?

■ Write the sermon focus—image, statement, or desired impact—in a short, declarative sentence. Even though the sermon may not be prepared for several weeks, the sermon focus will prove invaluable to the preacher, musician(s), and your whole worship planning team.

■ With the sermon focus in mind, the preacher may collect sermon ideas in the weeks ahead. Place those ideas in the worksheet file folders for each week.

See chapter 3 on "Preparing to Preach" for additional help.

4. Will there be Communion, a special emphasis, or a special service?
Enter on the worksheet any special emphasis, such as Service of the
Baptismal Covenant or installation of officers or the celebration of a
special day or anything else that may affect the service.

5. Schedule a planning meeting. Schedule a two-hour or longer meeting
with the musician(s) and the worship planning team. Remember to
schedule the meeting at least eight weeks before a season begins.

6. Prepare for a planning meeting.

■ Make copies of the worksheet for each service in the whole
season—complete with date, day, Scripture lessons and primary lesson,
sermon focus, and special emphasis.

■ Distribute the copies to all members of the planning team in advance.
Some efficient church offices will distribute in advance a computer
diskette containing the worksheet.

■ Before the planning meeting, the musician(s), pastor, and other
worship planners should prepare suggestions concerning hymns,
anthem(s), other worship leaders, and visuals on the worksheets
provided. Bring the printed-out worksheets to the planning meeting. At
the planning meeting, do the following:

7. Select hymns. Together, choose hymns for the services. In general, all
the hymns should reflect and enhance the Scripture of the day, the
sermon focus, or the service emphasis. For example, the first hymn may
be a hymn of praise, the second related to the sermon, and the third a
response to the Word, a communion hymn, or a hymn of sending forth.
Throughout *The United Methodist Book of Worship*, hymn suggestions
guide leaders to hymns they may not have considered otherwise.

One proven way to choose hymns is to use the indexes in the back of the
hymnal. As an example, for the Sundays of Advent, use the Index of Topics
and Categories (*UMH* 934-54) to find the Advent hymns. Look at each
hymn, read the commentary on each hymn in *The United Methodist Hymnal*
and make your selection. Or by using the Index of Scripture (*UMH* 923-26),
compare the Scripture lessons for the day related to particular hymns, or
use the complete hymn suggestions in the book of worship for each service
of worship. Unfamiliar texts and tunes need special study and preparation.
As you choose hymns, be sensitive to the meaning in each stanza. In some
hymns, stanzas may be omitted without damaging the whole text, but not
in all hymns. By simply saying, "Let us sing the first and last stanza,"
without first reading the text, you may rob the hymn of its full meaning and
effect on a service. Pick the stanzas best suited for a particular service.

■ Choose familiar and new hymns. While most hymns chosen for the services will be familiar to your congregation, it is important also to choose unfamiliar hymns to expand and deepen your congregation's experience of worship. You may want to introduce a new text by using an alternate tune. At the bottom of some hymns are suggestions for alternate tunes. The metrical index in the back of the hymnal (*UMH* 926) also enables you to determine what other tunes are likely to fit the words you want to sing. As you introduce new hymns, remember two wise sayings: (1) Never use only new hymns in any worship service, and (2) always teach a new hymn before using it.

In all of this work, plan for additional places that your congregation may sing in worship. The Basic Pattern avoids the "slot theory" of congregational worship—that is, hymns, anthems, and music appear in the same place every week. Instead, look at the flow and movement of each service and choose music accordingly. Ask what follows, what illumines, what carries out the theme, what interprets, and what fits best. For example, at the Gathering your congregation may have a mini-hymn festival, sing some old favorites, or rehearse unfamiliar music and the psalm response. During the Greeting, sing the opening stanza of "We Gather Together" (*UMH* 131) or "Morning Has Broken" (*UMH* 145). For Opening Prayer, sing "Just As I Am" (*UMH* 357). The Act of Praise may be one of several *Glorias* (*UMH* 82, 83, 72). The Prayer for Illumination may be "Open My Eyes" (*UMH* 454). Following the Gospel reading, sing one of the Alleuias (*UMH* 186, 486). Use the Index of Scripture (*UMH* 923-26) and sing one of the lessons. A hymn may lead into a sung prayer, such as "Lead Me, Lord" (*UMH* 473). Explore the different Doxologies at the Offering (*UMH* 94, 95). The Sending Forth has many possible musical options, such as "Blest Be the Tie That Binds" (*UMH* 557). A choral Amen may conclude the service (*UMH* 897-904). In An Order of Sunday Worship Using the Basic Pattern (*UMBOW* 16-32), see all the music listings for additional possibilities. Remember, the congregation can sing almost the entire service of worship.

■ Write down the hymn titles and tune names. See chapter 4 on "Planning for Congregational Singing" and chapter 5 on "Helping Your Congregation Sing" for additional help.

8. Choose anthem(s), service/communion music, and instrumental music. Based on the Scripture lessons, sermon focus, or the service emphasis, the musician(s) and pastor work together to create an environment of sound that enhances worship. Especially look at the service music suggestions throughout An Order of Sunday Worship Using the Basic Pattern (*UMBOW* 16-32) and the Music as Acts of Worship, a new set of service music in *UMBOW* 173-223.

The anthem(s) may be a hymn from the hymnal, particularly if the hymn is unfamiliar. Let your choir(s) sing the hymn and invite your congregation to follow in their hymnal. The *Music Supplement* to the hymnal is one excellent resource for such hymns/anthems.

■ The psalm of the day may be sung. The psalm of the day has a musical response printed at the top of each one in the hymnal. Prepare the instrumentalists and choir members to teach each psalm response to your congregation. The best time to teach the response is before the service, during the Gathering. See *Your Ministry of Singing the Psalms* among the Additional Resources for more help.

Both the Services of Word and Table and the Services of the Baptismal Covenant have musical responses (*UMH* 17-31 and 53-54). Prepare your musicians and singers to introduce and lead your congregation in singing these responses. *The Worship Resources of The United Methodist Hymnal*, chapter 3, describes ways of introducing this sacramental service music.

The subliminal teaching power of the opening voluntary (prelude), offertory, and closing voluntary (postlude) reinforces the recall of both old and new hymn tunes. Especially when teaching a new hymn, let the opening and closing music focus on the melody. Print the page number where the hymn can be found beside the name of the hymn arrangement so that your congregation can meditate on the text as they listen to the tune.

9. Choose singers and instrumentalists. Contact them well in advance. All musicians need time to practice and rehearse. Choose persons who can prepare well and who can offer adequate leadership. Do not overlook new talent. For example, encourage a young musician to introduce "Kum Ba Yah" or a children's choir to lead "Jesus Loves Me."

Enter your decisions on the worksheet.

10. Select other worship leaders. Lay liturgists, readers, acolytes, communion servers, ushers, and greeters are designated and trained.

Other participants—dancers, mimes, and other artists—could be chosen.

■ As leaders are chosen, intentionally include persons of all ages and conditions. Children, youth, and adults of all ages love to participate if asked and prepared. Persons with handicapping conditions can add greatly to your whole congregation's worship.

■ Enter the names and contact the people well in advance. When particular persons are chosen for a special service, give them a copy of the worksheet for the service to help them prepare.

11. Determine visuals. After the Scripture, sermon focus, hymns, music, and leaders have been chosen, determine the visual environment of worship. The introduction to each season of the Christian year in the *book of worship* and the worksheets in this book provide a few suggestions for visuals in worship.

■ Select the liturgical color(s). See the *Book of Worship,* pages 224 and 226, for a brief description of colors and their use throughout the Christian year.

Work with the flower coordinator, altar guild, or florist to select appropriate flowers or table settings. Plan to unwrap the Advent wreath, dust off the chrismons, construct a rugged cross, purchase a paschal candle, order a new communion cup and plate, or place an order for bread. Assign responsibilities.

Look again at your church's paraments, the choir's robes, the pastor's robe/alb and stoles. Which will go best with the Scripture at each service?

Enter this information on the worksheet.

WORSHIP PLANNING WORKSHEET

Date _____   Day in the Christian Year _____

Scriptures   Liturgical Color
First _____   Will there be Communion? _____
Psalm _____   Great Thanksgiving: *UMBOW* 54-80
Second _____   Special Emphasis or Special Service:
Gospel _____

Sermon Focus: _____

Hymns: _____

_____

_____

Anthems: _____

_____

Service/Communion Music: _____

_____

_____

Instrumental Music: _____

_____

Lay Liturgists/Readers: _____

Acolytes: _____

Other Participants: _____

Visuals: _____

Other Information: _____

3. PREPARING TO PREACH

Authentic biblical preaching, our first foundation stone, is again regaining prominence as a central task of all United Methodist pastors. Preaching enables the pastor to connect orally with the lives of those who hear. Good preaching demands personal devotion, serious study, adequate preparation, and major attention to a particular community of faith. Yet even more so, authentic preaching demands the eye-to-eye, heart-to-heart, life-to-life contact between the preacher and congregation. Throughout The United Methodist Church, prepared and imaginative preachers tell the biblical story, stories from the ages, stories from the lives of the congregation, and their own stories so that individuals and congregations may become a part of the divine narrative. Methods and style may and do vary in sermon preparation and delivery, but the essential requirement is that the Word becomes real.

As preachers prepare sermons, their starting point should always be the Bible. The living, breathing Word of God as embodied in the Old and New Testaments is the nucleus of all preaching. Thus the first step in preparing to preach is to be attentive to Scripture. Too often, preachers assume that they know the text, its message, and its direction. Also, too often, preachers depend on other persons and resources to tell about Scripture.

The following model is one pattern for listening directly to the living Word of God. The model is quite simple: Choose Scripture, read the text, listen for the Word, be silent, and then respond. This model will help you to attend to Scripture and make God's Word the center of each and every sermon and service of worship.

1. Plan ahead. Set aside at least half a day to plan.

■ Using a calendar, plan in advance for a whole season of the year at a time, at least eight weeks before the season begins. For example, no later than October 1 plan for Advent/Christmas/Epiphany. Likewise, no later than January 1 plan for the Lent/Easter/Pentecost cycle, and no later than April 1 plan for June, July, and August.

Determine which services will be held during each period. Certainly include every Sunday and then add any special services such as Christmas Eve, Ash Wednesday, or a revival or preaching mission. Review the contents page of *The United Methodist Book of Worship* (4-11) to remind yourself of all the special services that may be used.

■ Make a worksheet for each service. Enter the day and date of the service. Create a file folder for each service, in which you will collect all the resources you discover as you plan this service.

2. Choose Scripture. Three basic patterns facilitate choosing Scripture for preaching: (1) from the lectionary, (2) on the basis of a theme, or (3) by preaching through a book of the Bible. Each is appropriate within our Wesleyan tradition.

The *Revised Common Lectionary* (*UMBOW* 227-37) is one way to choose Scripture. This lectionary contains a three-year cycle of selected Old Testament, Psalm, Epistle, and Gospel readings for each Sunday and festival of the Christian year. A primary advantage of the lectionary is that it makes planning ahead simple.

A preacher may choose Scripture based on a theme or themes for a Sunday or for a whole season. Or a preacher may decide to use one book of the Bible and work through that book. These approaches enable the preacher to be intentional about the particular needs of a local congregation. If you use this model, be intentional in covering both the Old and the New Testaments over a period of time.

■ Enter one Scripture lesson on each worksheet.

Now, turn to the Scripture itself. Imagine that you are a juggler with three balls to juggle. The goal is to keep all three balls moving at the same time. As one ball is tossed, another drops from the sky, and a third is caught. So it is with preaching. In preparing to preach, you will juggle three worlds: the world of the Scripture, the world of the preacher (yourself), and the world of the community.

3. World of the living Word.

■ Read the text aloud. Read it with passion, as if you were reading it to your congregation.

■ Without exegetical help, answer the following questions:

1. Where is the event taking place? In what location did the Scripture arise?
2. When did it occur? What time and occasion gave rise to the Scripture?

3. Who are the characters? What people (and other parts of God's creation) are present, both seen and unseen?
4. What objects are present? What things, both visible and invisible, are a part of the narrative?
5. What is the sequence of scenes/themes? In what order do the events or ideas of the Scripture occur?
6. What seems strange or unexpected in the text?
7. What words appear to be most important? Are any striking nouns or verbs used?
8. Why was the Scripture written? What caused this passage to be written and saved by the community of faith?
9. Is there an invitation in the Scripture? Does the text have either an explicit or implicit invitation to the audience?

Enter your answers on the worksheet.

4. World of the preacher.

■ Read the Scripture aloud. Use the voices of the different characters in the text.

■ Answer the following questions, relating yourself to the text:

1. With which characters do I identify? With which character am I the most comfortable? With which character am I the most uncomfortable?
2. When have I experienced this Scripture? Which of my life experiences parallel this text?
3. What is (was) my reaction? What feelings and thoughts arose out of this situation?
4. To what does God invite me through this text? How does this Scripture call me?

■ Enter appropriate responses on the worksheet.

5. World of the community.

■ Listen to the Scripture as would a member of your congregation.

■ Answer the following questions, relating your community to the Scripture (be careful to include the church universal in your community and not limited yourself just to the people in your local congregation):

1. When does (did) this community experience an event similar to this text as individuals? Are there persons in this community who live (lived) this story?
2. When does (did) this community as a corporate body experience a similar event?

3. When does (did) this community experience this Scripture through its oral tradition? What shared stories in the community parallel the text?
4. When does (did) my community experience this event through its culture? What movies, television programs, magazines, and books (familiar to your community) parallel this Scripture?
5. What is (was) my community's reaction to this event? How do (did) people respond?
6. How does God invite my community through this text? What grace does God offer my community through this Scripture?

■ Enter each of your responses on the worksheet.

Now, juggling the three worlds of the Scripture, the preacher, and the community, you may need to do further work. Some approaches follow.

6. Research.

■ Review all the questions and answers you gave above.

■ Ask the following questions:

1. What more do I need to know about the Scripture? What perceptions do I need to reexamine?
2. What more do I need to know about myself? What perceptions do I need to evaluate?
3. What more do I need to know about my community? What perceptions do I need to evaluate?

■ Third, look for answers to the above questions and write these answers on the worksheet.

7. Choose the sermon focus. The sermon focus—the basic image, statement, or desired impact that guides the sermon—will give direction to the service.

■ Write the sermon focus—image, statement, or desired impact—in a short, declarative sentence. Even though the sermon may not be prepared for several weeks, the sermon focus will prove invaluable. With the sermon focus in mind, you can collect sermon ideas in the weeks ahead. Place those ideas in the worksheet file folder.

Now, you may choose the special services; select hymns; choose anthems, service music, and instrumental music; select other worship leaders; and determine visuals. See chapter 2, "Planning Worship," in this book to aid you in this work.

Place all of your information in a file folder for each service within a season of the Christian year. The file folder will hold all the resources for preaching and worship that you discover in the weeks and months ahead.

PREPARING TO PREACH WORKSHEET

Date: _____ Day of the Christian Year: _____

Scripture: _____

World of the Living Word:

    Where:_____

    When:_____

    Characters:_____

    Objects:_____

    Sequence:_____

    The Unexpected:_____

    Words:_____

    Why:_____

    Invitation:_____

World of the Preacher:

    Characters:_____

    Experiences:_____

    Reactions:_____

    Invitation:_____

World of the Community:

    Personal Experiences:_____

    Community Experiences:_____

    Oral Traditions:_____

    Culture:_____

    Reactions:_____

    Invitation:_____

Sermon Focus:

4. PLANNING FOR CONGREGATIONAL SINGING

John and Charles Wesley knew the importance of music and integrated hymn singing in every facet of their revival movement. Congregational singing is no less important today. The responsibility of singing is on every leader of worship in your congregation, with your help, and together your congregation can continue the tradition of being "a singing church."

Your congregation sings because the hymns and music teach about the Bible and the world. Through singing, your congregation learns about God's abundant grace and steadfast love, Jesus' life and teachings, and the ongoing reality of the Holy Spirit. Hymns express social concerns, past and present; give insights to peoples from different experiences, different lands, and different struggles; and can be a statement of faith shared by your whole congregation. Singing unifies a body of individuals into one community.

Too often, however, congregational singing may be taken for granted in your congregation; it may not be well planned and prepared, and it is often poorly led and supported. Yet your United Methodist congregation can be a singing congregation. How will you plan to integrate the hymnal and book of worship into your congregation's worship experience?

Good congregational singing does not just happen. While people love to sing, the musicians and pastors in your congregation must intentionally work together to strengthen congregational singing. Planning for vital singing requires self-evaluation by your congregation, serious study, specific standards, and a clear course of action.

1. Begin with your congregation. What do your people love to sing? What do they know? What are they willing to learn? It is better not to assume that you know the answers to these questions before you ask. And congregations change so rapidly in our culture that frequent asking is a good way to discipline your listening skills.

Observe your congregation and gather information. Go through old bulletins of your past worship services. Remember the hymns people have requested. Recall which hymns you suspect everybody loves but have not sung. Write down which hymns are in the current repertoire of your congregation.

■ Open a copy of *The United Methodist Hymnal*. Put a check beside each hymn you believe your congregation already knows.

■ Take a hymn survey. Ask a variety of persons within your membership to look at every hymn in the hymnal. Be certain to include longtime and new members, youth, young adults, and persons from different backgrounds. Involve members of your choir as well as people who do not like to sing.

The people participating in the survey may work individually or together as a Sunday school class youth meeting, or as a Sunday evening program group. Because many people do not know hymns just by their title, work with an actual copy of the hymnal for each person rather than a list of hymns. Ask each person to mark the hymnal (in pencil) using a rating system: three stars for a favorite hymn; two stars for a familiar hymn that may be sung without further help; one star for a hymn not known but desirable to learn. Have as many people as possible rate the hymns in order to increase the reliability of the information.

Finally, your musician and pastor together should collate the material, take averages of the ratings, and make pencil marks in one copy of *The United Methodist Hymnal*. Rate each hymn with one, two, or three stars. This one hymnal will become the most valuable resource for congregational singing. Use this hymnal every week. After every service of worship, open this hymnal and write down beside each hymn the date on which it was sung. Be prepared to change the number of stars; your congregation's repertoire will change, and your planning must change with your congregation. If a new pastor is appointed or a musician hired, this book should be passed on to the new person to aid him or her in worship planning. Nevertheless, it is a good idea to do a hymn survey every few years and begin fresh.

2. Interpret the survey. Once you have taken the hymn survey, interpret your congregation's repertoire by asking these questions: Why do the people love what they do? Why do they not appreciate other hymns? What is the favorite style of music of our congregation: gospel, spiritual, contemporary, or classic? What style of singing does this congregation enjoy: full accompaniment, piano, or a cappella?

Be sensitive to your congregation's investment in their hymns. Based on your hymn survey and your own insights, you may be able to anticipate which hymns your congregation wants to sing. For example, one congregation may be open to singing hymns from a wide variety of ethnic cultures while another congregation may want to emphasize contemporary and children's hymns.

The United Methodist Hymnal could become your closest companion in a worship and devotional life. Some leaders each day read aloud one hymn and let it become a prayer. Some learn by heart one new hymn every week. Some reflect on the history of each tune and text. A useful guide for this kind of exercise is *The Hymns of The United Methodist Hymnal*.

3. Determine standards. Having evaluated your congregation's hymn singing and studied the hymnal itself, it is appropriate to set standards for your congregation. How will you choose hymns for congregational worship? How will your congregation use its voice in worship? How much should your congregation sing?

While there are many criteria that can be set by worship leaders of your congregation, at least four standards are encouraged for most congregations.

A. Provide more opportunities for congregational singing. Look at the acts of worship within the services and make note of those that may be sung by the people. *The United Methodist Book of Worship* suggests ways the whole or parts of every service can be sung. Work intentionally to increase congregational singing.

B. Let the Word of God be the nucleus and focus of all congregational singing. The Word of God read, proclaimed, and heard should primarily determine what music, hymns, and psalms are chosen and sung in worship. For this to work in worship, pastors and musicians will learn to plan ahead. Invaluable in all this work will be the Index of Scripture (*UMH* 923-26) in the hymnal and an expanded Index of Scripture in *The Hymns of The United Methodist Hymnal* (pp. 273-79).

C. Make your music and hymnody more diverse. In every congregation, women, men, and children come with a variety of needs and gifts. Your music can affirm that rich diversity so as to include those who enjoy highly structured worship as well as those who like charismatic, Southern gospel, African American, and evangelical worship styles. When the hymns encompass the multiplicity of races and cultures, then we realize how God's love is offered to all people and races. An obtainable goal for any congregation is to learn at least one new hymn a year from each of the cultures represented in the hymnal outside of your congregation's dominant repertoire: African American, Hispanic, Asian American, Native American, and Anglo-American. All ages are present in your congregation, which means hymns for older adults, children, and youth should be included. *The United Methodist Hymnal* and *The United Methodist Book of Worship* witness to the unique spiritual gifts of many peoples; encourage your congregation to share these gifts as mediators of God's grace to all the cultures of the world.

D. *Increase your congregation's repertoire slowly and steadily.* Attempting to learn too many new hymns too quickly will frustrate you and your congregation. Carefully and wisely choose a variety of hymns, integrating them into your congregation's repertoire over a period of time. For example, you can help your congregation to learn one new hymn for each major season of the Christian year.

These four standards—encourage more congregational singing, focus on the Word of God, affirm diversity, and increase your congregation's repertoire—may stimulate your work in setting additional standards for your congregation.

4. Chart a course. Prepare long-range plans. Knowing your congregation, understanding the hymnal, and setting standards are the necessary steps prior to charting your course and implementing goals to strengthen congregational singing. As you make plans, three key elements are vital to any successful work.

A. *Evaluate the changes necessary to encourage congregational singing.* Will a song leader help your congregation sing better? How can you better support your congregation and choir? Have the resources needed for vocal and instrumental support of congregational singing been provided?

B. *Teach your congregation.* Use every opportunity in your congregation's life to teach about the hymnal, including the Sunday school and other educational settings. Musicians and pastors working together with teachers can inform and bring excitement to the educational setting. This may be the time to reintroduce vital singing in your Sunday school.

C. *Seek and gain congregational support.* Musicians and pastors, along with teachers, can help you excite the whole congregation about a new emphasis on singing. Tell people they can sing! Describe hymns in your worship bulletins and newsletters. Create a hymn bulletin board that receives contributions from everyone in your congregation. Work with your Administrative Council or Administrative Board and Council on Ministries to gain their support. Worship and sing during church business meetings (possibly using one of the Orders of Daily Praise and Prayer; see chap. 18). Worship and sing during every congregational gathering, including fellowship dinners.

Now, with a better understanding of your congregation, having prepared yourself and having set standards, you may begin making plans to strengthen congregational singing.

5. HELPING YOUR CONGREGATION SING

Having planned for your congregation's singing, how will you introduce new music to your congregation? What can you do to help your congregation sing?

As leaders of worship strengthen the congregational singing in your church, consider three critical factors: the quality of the vocal leadership, the strength of the instrumental support, and the pattern of introducing new hymns and music to your congregation. In this era when churches are turning away from hymnals to scripture choruses on an overhead projector, we have a clear opportunity to teach and train worshipers to sing both hymns and choruses. An intentional effort is required.

1. Provide firm vocal leadership. Superior vocal leadership is critical for congregational singing. Several strategies will aid in providing such leadership.

■ Rehearse your congregation and Sunday school classes before worship. Many Sunday school classes share in hymn singing as part of their time together. Visit Sunday school classes for all ages and rehearse hymns for worship. The members will become leaders among the rest of the congregation and with encouragement will be strong advocates of congregational participation. Teach new hymns and service music to your congregation during the gathering before worship. If announcements are a part of the gathering time, introduce the new hymn following the last announcement. Immediately after the hymn is taught, the opening music may begin. A song leader or cantor may lead hymns in your congregation. A song leader's presence at the front of your congregation is helpful for any who need visual as well as musical leadership. This person may be the choir director, pastor, or another person from the congregation. Your song leader should have a strong voice and a clear conducting style that invites active participation.

2. Provide strong instrumental leadership. Congregational singing often depends on the quality of the music played by your instrumentalists. The piano, organ, guitar, or other instrument played by a leader of worship with a strong sense of rhythm is a prerequisite to vital singing. Several suggestions will help improve this leadership.

■ Ensure that your accompanist knows the music well in advance of the service. The accompanist should be given a list of all music at least a week in advance. Discuss the tempos and registrations for different stanzas with the accompanist. Correct rhythms and tempos are crucial. Hymns played too slowly may lead to lethargic singing; hymns played too fast may discourage singing. The organist or pianist should make an effort to reflect the hymn text through organ registration and pianistic color. The textures and moods of stanzas can be complemented with creative preparation.

■ Use other instruments to enhance a musical setting; a flute, a violin, a clarinet, or a trumpet may highlight the melody. Instead of an organ, use a piano or a guitar, or use rhythm instruments such as drums, maracas, finger cymbals, and triangle to add rhythmic interest. Handbells also provide wonderful accompaniment to hymns.

3. Introduce new hymns. *The United Methodist Hymnal* has a total of 624 hymns and canticles. *The United Methodist Book of Worship* has 51 musical acts of worship. Of those hymns and canticles your congregation may use fewer than 100 over the next several years. Most of those hymns and musical acts of worship will be current favorites, yet every congregation desires the opportunity to learn new hymns. How can this be accomplished? Teaching and introducing new hymns takes planning, constant reinforcing, and patience. The following method is one way to introduce new hymns to your congregation.

■ First, your musician or pastor must learn and know the hymn before he or she can effectively teach it! Then, teach all your worship leaders. This includes the instrumentalists, director, choir, pastor, and everyone else in front of your congregation. If the hymn is worth introducing to the congregation, it is worth the worship leaders' time to learn it. Especially your pastor must be willing to communicate the value of congregational singing and enthusiastically participate in the singing of all hymns, old and new. Others who may learn new hymns before the congregation gathers are Sunday school classes, fellowship groups (United Methodist Women, Men, Youth), or prayer and Bible study groups.

■ Second, encourage a strong, energetic, positive person to lead your congregation in singing. In most cases, your song leader will introduce new hymns because the congregation is accustomed to this person's leadership in worship and respects his or her knowledge and authority. In many congregations, however, the music leader is both choir director and organist. In this case, it may be difficult to introduce a new hymn or service music from behind the organ console. Instead, a strong singer with a pleasant voice, clear enunciation, and strong sense of rhythm should be asked to introduce the new hymn. This leader should stand in front of your congregation and with a positive attitude motivate the congregation. Nothing diminishes a congregation's enthusiasm for singing more quickly than feeling apprehensive about what and when they should sing. The best approach is one of gentle patience, constant encouragement, and a dash of humor. Rehearsal of the accompanist and music leader is necessary before rehearsing your congregation.

■ Third, sharing information with your congregation about new and old hymns will help them identify with the hymn. When using *The Hymns of The United Methodist Hymnal*, which includes a paragraph on each hymn found in your hymnal, decide what you will share with the congregation when you introduce a hymn. Read the paragraph and the Scripture passage(s) on which the text is based, highlighting specific stanzas that point to that passage. Explain to the congregation where the hymn comes in the service and how it relates to what precedes or follows it. Tell them why you think the hymn is worth learning and why you enjoy it. Have the accompanist play the hymn through once as the congregation listens or hums and follows in their hymnals.

■ Fourth, have the song leader sing the first stanza as the congregation listens and hums; or have the choir (adult, children, or youth) sing the first stanza. Add an instrument to highlight the melody. Have the congregation sing a stanza with the song leader or choir. If it sounds shaky, try a third stanza. If a specific part of the hymn is troublesome, rehearse that spot before singing the hymn again.

■ Fifth, when the congregation sings the hymn in worship, use the choir to reinforce the melody line. Reserve part-singing for a time when the congregation sings more confidently, or when the choir sings alone.

■ Finally, use the opening voluntary (prelude), offertory, and closing voluntary (postlude) to reinforce new hymn tunes. Organ and piano arrangements for hymn tunes can be found in most music stores, or you or your accompanist may create a free harmonization. *The Music Supplement* to the hymnal is also invaluable. Other times for reinforcing new hymns are at gatherings such as fellowship dinners, Bible studies, and church meetings. These are excellent times to sing favorites and learn new hymns. Use the same pattern suggested for Sunday morning.

Another method of introducing new hymns is through special programs. A Sunday evening or morning hymn festival is a great way of celebrating the rich hymnody found in our hymnal. To organize a hymn festival, simply decide on a theme (a season of the Christian year, such as Advent; hymns written by women; Wesleyan hymns; American hymns; or other theme); choose five to ten hymns (both old and new); intersperse the hymns with prayers and Scripture readings (see the Indexes of Topics and Scripture); prepare the choir to sing a hymn arrangement; designate different stanzas to different groups (choir, congregation, men, women, youth, children, Sunday school classes); prepare visuals relating to the theme; and ask persons in your congregation to participate in the leadership. For assistance, see *Your Ministry of Planning and Leading Hymn Festivals* in the Additional Resources.

6. HOLY COMMUNION

A major liturgical achievement of both *The United Methodist Hymnal* and *The United Methodist Book of Worship* is the reclaiming of our strong Wesleyan eucharistic tradition. Once again, United Methodists center their worship on the Word preached and celebration of the Word around the Table.

The Lord's Supper is the primary means of grace in the theology of John Wesley. In this sacrament, words, signs, and action combine to present the full power of God's grace:

> *Is not the eating of that bread, and the drinking of that cup, the outward, visible means, whereby God conveys into our souls all that spiritual grace? Let all, therefore, who truly desire the grace of God eat of that bread, and drink of that cup?"* (Wesley, *Works XII*, p. 147)

In eating the bread and drinking from the cup, the people of faith are in the living presence of Christ Jesus.

John Wesley affirmed that Holy Communion had four functions. The holy meal was a memorial, a means of grace, a stimulus to future hope, and a sacrifice. Because of its multiple functions, Wesley argued that Holy Communion was the richest presentation of the full gospel. He and Charles stated this view in their hymn "The Means of Grace":

> Fasting He doth, and Hearing bless,
> And Prayer can much avail,
> Good Vessels all to draw the Grace
> Out of Salvation's Well.
>
> But none like this Mysterious Rite
> Which dying Mercy gave,
> Can draw forth all His promis'd Might
> And all His Will to save.

This is the richest Legacy
Thou hast on Man bestow'd'
Here chiefly, LORD, we feed on Thee
And drink thou precious Blood.
(John Rattenbury, *The Eucharist Hymns of John and Charles Wesley* [London: Epworth, 1948], p. 207)

While *The United Methodist Hymnal* includes the four most common congregational services of Holy Communion, entitled Services of Word and Table, *The United Methodist Book of Worship* supplements these services in a wide variety of ways. This commentary will concentrate on how the *Book of Worship* supplements the services found in the hymnal, and how to use these two resources together.

Following the patterns established by the hymnal, *The United Methodist Book of Worship* includes the following worship resources for Holy Communion:

A Service of Word and Table I
Introduction to A Service of Word and Table II
Introduction to A Service of Word and Table III
Introduction to The Great Thanksgiving: Musical Settings
A Service of Word and Table IV (Traditional Methodist and E.U.B.)
A Service of Word and Table V
  (With Persons Who Are Sick or Homebound)
The Great Thanksgiving for Advent
The Great Thanksgiving for Christmas Eve, Day, or Season
The Great Thanksgiving for New Year, Epiphany, Baptism of the Lord,
  or Covenant Reaffirmation
The Great Thanksgiving for Early in Lent
The Great Thanksgiving for Later in Lent
The Great Thanksgiving for Holy Thursday Evening
The Great Thanksgiving for Easter Day or Season
The Great Thanksgiving for the Day of Pentecost
The Great Thanksgiving for the Season after Pentecost
The Great Thanksgiving for World Communion Sunday
The Great Thanksgiving for All Saints and Memorial Occasions
The Great Thanksgiving for Thanksgiving Day or for the Gift of Food
An Alternative Great Thanksgiving for General Use
A Brief Great Thanksgiving for General Use

SERVICE OF WORD AND TABLE I

In both *The United Methodist Hymnal* and *The United Methodist Book of Worship*, A Service of Word and Table I provides a complete service of preaching and Holy Communion built upon The Basic Pattern of Worship. It provides your congregation one complete service of worship when the congregation wishes to read the entire service with minimal alternatives. It requires only that the hymns and Scripture lessons be read aloud or posted on hymn boards. You may also use this service when your people need a service that is largely pre-planned and has minimal options. No worship bulletin is needed when you use this service.

The only difference between the service in the hymnal and the *Book of Worship* is that the *Book of Worship* provides a few additional rubrics and refers the leaders to other pages in the book for optional acts of worship and pastoral suggestions.

SERVICES OF WORD AND TABLE II AND III

While *The United Methodist Hymnal* includes the two Services of Word and Table II and III (*UMH* 12-16), *The United Methodist Book of Worship* includes only a brief introduction to each. In each case, the services are clear and simple, and they may be enriched by using one of the additional Prayers of Great Thanksgiving for Holy Communion found in the book of worship (*UMBOW* 54-80).

In each case, the services are simple and flexible and may be used in a great variety of settings and occasions in your congregation. A Service of Word and Table II is most similar to the brief service of Holy Communion found in the hymnals of our former denominations. A Service of Word and Table III is the most flexible and is easily adapted to many particular needs, especially for congregations who do not wish to sing their responses in the Prayer of Great Thanksgiving.

For these two services, your congregation would only use their hymnals, and you would not need to reprint the service in your worship bulletin. Simply announce or display the Scripture lessons and hymns, and then have your congregation follow the service in the hymnal. With either of the services, however, you may print a worship bulletin with the Service of the Word, including Scripture lessons and hymn numbers, and then conclude the Service of the Table with everyone following the service in the hymnal through the end of the service.

THE GREAT THANKSGIVING MUSICAL SETTINGS

One of the most exciting sections of *The United Methodist Hymnal* is "The Great Thanksgiving: Musical Settings" (*UMH* 17-25). In each Prayer of Great Thanksgiving, there are three congregational responses that may be sung: "Holy, holy, holy Lord . . . " (the *Sanctus* and *Benedictus*);

"Christ has died . . . " (the Memorial Acclamation), and the Great Amen. When your congregation sings these responses, they enhance the whole tone and character of the eucharistic prayer.

These musical responses all follow the basic outline of the Prayer of Great Thanksgiving, and the lead-in lines are the same as you will find throughout the hymnal and the book of worship. The pastor may use any of the Prayer of Great Thanksgiving found in the hymnal or book of worship with any of these five musical settings.

When you use one of these musical settings, you might designate it in your worship bulletin in the following way:

Taking of the Bread and Cup
The Great Thanksgiving (Musical Setting A, p. 17)
The Lord's Prayer
Breaking the Bread
Giving the Bread and Cup

Musical Setting A is very simple and joyous. Because of its familiar beginning, it is quite accessible to congregations and may be the first musical setting your congregation will learn.

Musical Setting B is also easy for your congregation to sing. Let the choir or a solo song leader sing one phrase, and then have the congregation simply repeat the musical phrase. If you choose this setting, the pastor and choir or song leader should rehearse together to be sure that they each know their lead-in lines. With such rehearsal, the people will not even have to look at the printed page as they follow you in singing this musical setting. A children's or youth choir is ideal for teaching this setting to the congregation.

Musical Setting C is a rich German piece that may be sung in four-part harmony. It received wide early use in the hymnal *Sampler* and has been used in many congregations. At the first service in which you use this setting, let the choir sing it by themselves. The next time you use this musical setting, let the choir lead the congregation, and invite the members of the congregation to participate as they are comfortable. After one or two times, everyone will be able to sing this music.

Musical Setting D is the only setting in a minor key. Especially during Advent and Lent the congregation may wish to sing this music. With a little work, it may also be sung in a call-and-response form. Let the choir or a song leader sing one phrase, and then have the congregation repeat the line.

Musical Setting E is majestic and rich. While it is more complex and demanding than the other settings, the congregation may enjoy it during Christmas and Easter. At the first service in which you use this setting, let your youth or adult choir sing it by themselves. The next time you use the musical setting, let the choir lead the congregation. After one or two times, everyone will be able to sing this music.

The congregation can sing all five of these musical settings, and each one will greatly enhance your services of Holy Communion.

SERVICE OF WORD AND TABLE IV (TRADITIONAL METHODIST AND E.U.B.)

Both *The United Methodist Hymnal* (*UMH* 26-31) and *The United Methodist Book of Worship* (*UMBOW* 41-50) include a traditional text (including music) for Holy Communion from the services of the former denominations that became our Church. The service is an adaption of the service of Holy Communion in *The Book of Common Prayer* of the Church of England, which John Wesley sent to the American Methodists in 1784. Lent is an ideal season for the use of this service in your congregation.

The *Book of Worship* expands the service found in the hymnal (which begins with the Invitation) by including all of this historic service. Everything beginning with the Invitation is the same in both the hymnal and the *Book of Worship*. Like all the other services of Holy Communion, it is a complete service of both Word and Table.

You might use this service in the following ways. First, using the book of worship resources, create a worship bulletin that includes elements from the Entrance and Proclamation and Response, such as Scripture lessons, hymns, and prayers. Then, list in your bulletin: HOLY COMMUNION—page 26. The congregation may then follow in their hymnals through the end of the service. The pastor, however, will need to continue using the book of worship for the Prayer of Great Thanksgiving in order to add the preface appropriate to the season of the Christian year.

Because this is clearly the longest and most confessional service in our tradition, its use is on the decline throughout our denomination. It remains, however, a vital part of our tradition.

SERVICE OF WORD AND TABLE V (WITH PERSONS WHO ARE SICK OR HOME BOUND)

Since the time of the early church, Holy Communion has been brought to sick and shut-in persons unable to be present at congregational worship. This service encourages your congregation's worship to extend beyond the Dismissal with Blessing until everyone in the congregation's community of faith has shared together in the holy meal.

This service was not included in *The United Methodist Hymnal* because it does not involve a full congregation using hymnals. It has been included, however, in *The United Methodist Book of Worship* (*UMBOW* 51-53). Consider several nuances as you use this service in your congregation.

1. *The service is meant to be flexible and personal.* While a specific text is given for use, the service should be adapted to the setting (a home, hospital, or institutional setting) and by no means read straight from the book. Likewise, make it specific to the persons receiving the sacrament. Use their names often, touch them with your hands, and allow them to participate as much as possible. Use familiar language, hymns, and prayers whenever possible.

2. *The book of worship allows and encourages laypersons to distribute the consecrated bread and cup to persons away from the church building who are sick or homebound.* This provision was explicitly agreed to by the 1992 General Conference. This should greatly expand the possibility of sharing Holy Communion more frequently with the sick and shut-ins in your congregation. This ministry of the laity, however, does have several conditions: laypersons should conduct this ministry with the supervision of the pastor, including a brief period of training on how to use the service; they should serve the elements as soon as possible following a service of Holy Communion as an extension of the service (such as on a Sunday afternoon); and they should omit The Great Thanksgiving Prayer, as this Prayer is said only by ordained clergy or a local pastor in charge of a congregation.

This service will enrich your congregation's ministry of Holy Communion in many wonderful ways. And the sick and homebound persons in your congregation will be more closely united with God.

SEASONAL AND ALTERNATIVE GREAT THANKSGIVINGS

The United Methodist Book of Worship includes thirteen additional Prayers of Great Thanksgiving for Holy Communion (*UMBOW* 54-80), all of which may be used in your local congregation. Other Prayers of Great Thanksgiving are found in other sections of the *Book of Worship*, such as in the Healing Services. Earlier versions of these prayers are found in the books *At the Lord's Table* and *Holy Communion*, both authored chiefly by Hoyt Hickman. They include the major festival days in the Christian year, and contain two prayers (A Brief Thanksgiving for General Use and An Alternative Great Thanksgiving) that break new ground in the use of inclusive language.

Only the pastor needs these prayers in the *Book of Worship* at the

Communion Table. Your congregation may best follow along using A Service of Word and Table III (*UMH* 15-16) or one of the musical settings for Holy Communion (*UMH* 17-25). Any of the five musical settings may be used with any one of these Prayers of Great Thanksgiving, but try to match the musical character of the people's responses with the eucharistic prayer (such as using Musical Setting D during Lent). While the *Book of Worship* also recommends the use of A Service of Word and Table II (*UMH* 13-15), this is somewhat more awkward for the congregation. The lead-in lines in each Prayer of Great Thanksgiving are exactly the same, and the congregation will know exactly where to pick up and either say or sing their parts of the Prayer of Great Thanksgiving.

The Prayers of Great Thanksgiving in the book of worship, however, are not exhaustive of all the Prayers of Great Thanksgiving you may use. Ideally, they should inspire you to create your own unique Prayers of Great Thanksgiving, such as a Prayer of Great Thanksgiving for a Homecoming Service or Revival. Encourage your pastor to begin using extempore Prayers of Great Thanksgiving. As long as you keep the basic pattern of the Prayer of Great Thanksgiving and use the same lead-in lines for your congregation, this will make the Prayer of Great Thanksgiving even more specific to the day and to the occasion in your local congregation.

ADDITIONAL PASTORAL SUGGESTIONS

In addition to the particular suggestions given for the above services, the following ideas will enrich the practice of the Lord's Supper in your congregation:

1. Serve more frequently. If you currently celebrate the holy meal quarterly, move toward a monthly celebration. If you now celebrate monthly, move toward weekly observance. Celebrate the meal in relation to the seasons and days of the Christian year: the First Sunday of Advent, Christmas Eve, Christmas Day, the Day of Epiphany, the First Sunday in Lent, Passion/Palm Sunday, Holy Thursday, Easter Vigil, Day of Easter, Day of Pentecost, and All Saints Day. (See *UMBOW* 54-80 for thirteen Prayers of Great Thanksgiving for Holy Communion centered on the Christian year.) Not all church members will endorse this frequency, but a large number will. Some churches add a second service for those who prefer weekly Communion. Also, notice that the book of worship encourages Holy Communion during weddings, funerals, healing services, and a number of other occasions.

2. Vary the worship settings. In addition to your sanctuary, a fellowship hall, a garden, a home, or a camp are all excellent locations for Communion, and each will add a fresh dimension to the service.

3. Always center the worship space on the Communion table. If you have an altar/table against a wall or the pulpit, pull the altar/table away from the wall or pulpit (so that the celebrant can stand behind the table), or use another free-standing, rectangular table for the celebration. Clear away anything that obstructs your congregation from seeing the table, and clear the table of all clutter, such as a flower arrangement. Let your people see clearly the bread and the cup.

4. Coordinate the colors to the season. While the linens lying flat on the table are always white, the paraments, as well as the stoles and banners in your congregation, should be those of the Christian year (see *UMBOW* 226 for color suggestions).

5. Four actions. Most important, let all four actions of Holy Communion—take, bless, break, and give—be visible to the entire congregation.

■ *Take:* Taking the bread and cup. Use a whole loaf of bread sitting on a plate (paten) and grape juice or wine in a large cup (chalice). Encourage members of your congregation to make and prepare the elements. Bring in the elements with the offering of the day. Encourage the people who make the elements (for example a family with children) to bring the elements forward.

■ *Bless:* Praying the Prayer of Great Thanksgiving. The pastor should stand behind the table, facing the people. While standing, the pastor should assume the *orans* prayer posture (head erect or lifted, arms flexed and to the side, palms forward). Encourage your congregation to stand. Follow the specific rubrics in the book of worship about where to raise or lower the hands. Because there is no one way of using these sign-acts, choose and use actions most comfortable for you. Use the appropriate Prayer of Great Thanksgiving, but be flexible and also use extempore Prayers of Great Thanksgiving that are specific to the service and to the congregation. Sing the congregational responses to the Prayer: the *Sanctus* and *Benedictus* ("Holy, holy, holy . . . "), the Memorial Acclamation ("Christ has died, Christ is risen, Christ will come again"), and the Great Amen (*UMH* 17-25). Conclude with the Lord's Prayer sung or spoken (*UMH* 270, 271, 894-96).

■ *Break:* Breaking the Bread. The pastor lifts the bread and breaks it, with or without words. Everyone in your congregation should see this action.

The pastor then raises the cup, with or without words. Again, everyone should see the action.

■ *Give:* Giving the bread and cup. Invite everyone to the table, yet allow persons to abstain without embarrassment. If you have persons with handicapping conditions, either serve them at their seats or make the altar area accessible to them; ask them to decide how they wish to receive. Encourage your ushers to be gentle guides, not line marshals, aiding your congregation to come to the table. To assist new members and visitors, explain who is invited to receive and how Communion is to be received, either in your worship bulletin or as an announcement before the service. Encourage children of all ages to receive. Encourage the baptized leaders of your congregation to assist in the distribution of the elements. Encourage your people to receive bread by placing their right hand on their left palm, creating a small cross or a throne for the gift.

While giving the bread and cup is primarily nonverbal, a simple phrase such as "The body of Christ for you, *(person's name)* or "The blood of Christ for you, *(person's name)* enhances the serving. While giving the bread, maintain eye contact with the people being served, and do not hesitate to touch gently the recipient.

6. Consider congregational singing. The use of music dramatically heightens the quality and intensity of the Lord's Supper. Whether the congregation sings during the serving of the sacrament is a decision to be made by the pastor and the worship committee. If you do sing hymns, be sure to choose enough so that you do not run out of hymns before everyone receives. Choose hymns that match the tone of the sacrament—penitential hymns during Lent and joyful hymns on Easter and Pentecost (see the hymns suggested in *UMBOW* 30-31).

7. Restore order. Set the table in order when all have been served. Clean the cup and pick up the crumbs.

The remaining elements may be set aside for later distribution to the sick or others unable to attend. Clergy and laity may participate in this ministry (see Service of Word and Table V, *UMBOW* 51). Or the remaining elements may be wholly consumed by the pastor and others as a sign of respect for the elements. Or the remaining elements may be returned to the earth, a biblical gesture of worship (see 2 Sam. 23:16) and an ecological symbol today. Whatever you choose to do with the remaining elements should express stewardship of God's gifts and respect for the purpose these elements have served.

STYLES OF DISTRIBUTION

Communion services in Advent, Lent, and other times of penitence (such as revivals) suggest a style of distribution that encourages the people to kneel and be humble in the presence of God. You might teach your congregation the full Communion service from the Anglican tradition (Word and Table IV in *UMH* and *UMBOW*), keeping in mind that the mood of that service is more penitential and confessional than the other services of Word and Table.

Each of the following styles enables your people to be more reflective as they receive and meditate on the Lord's Supper. On these days, while the people move quietly during the distribution, your choir may sing anthems or hymns. As a church grows larger, the worship committee should evaluate how much time is available for serving the whole congregation.

■ **1. Pastors and lay servers stand in front of the Communion rail.** People form a single line, coming one by one to the servers, and kneel (or stand), receive the elements, and then either proceed to the Communion rail to kneel and pray, returning to their seats when they wish, or return immediately to their seats after receiving for a time of prayer and meditation. This style of distribution takes the least amount of time of these three methods.

■ **2. Pastors and lay servers stand in pairs behind the Communion rail.** Individuals, when they desire, come to the Communion rail and kneel. A pair of servers immediately provides the elements. Individuals may then remain for silent prayers as long as they wish and then return to their seats. When one person leaves the rail, another takes that place, and the pattern is repeated. This style requires a longer time for distribution.

■ **3. Pastors and servers stand behind the Communion rail.** People come by tables (small groups) and kneel together; all receive the elements at the same time, hear a blessing, rise, and return to their seats. Then another table comes forward. This style takes the longest time of any method of distribution.

Communion services at Christmas, Easter, and other joyful times (such as All Saints Day) suggest a style of distribution that encourages the mingling and free movement of people. Each of the following styles enables people to rejoice in the Lord's Supper, and in each style, the Lord's Supper is distributed in a relatively short time. The whole congregation may sing hymns during the distribution.

■ **1. Pastors and servers stand at the table,** divide the elements, and place them on trays. Servers then pass the trays from person to person, pew to pew, with each person serving the one seated next to him or her. This method takes the least amount of time.

■ **2. Pastors and servers divide into pairs** and stand at several places in the worship area. People then come, stand, and receive from the servers closest to them. People then return to their seats. This method takes a longer time.

■ **3. Pastors and servers stand at one place** at the front of the sanctuary. People form a single line, come, stand, receive, and return to their seats. This method takes the most time of these three methods.

For further help with Holy Communion, see *The Worship Resources of The United Methodist Hymnal* in Additional Resources.

7. BAPTISM

Like Holy Communion, a major liturgical achievement of both *The United Methodist Hymnal* and *The United Methodist Book of Worship* is the reclaiming of our strong Wesleyan theology of baptism. Once again, United Methodists remember that Christians are created through the sacrament of baptism.

Baptism, within our Wesleyan tradition, is a sure and effectual means of grace. John Wesley declared that when faithful sponsors presented a child or when an adult came on profession of faith, God bestowed through baptism five benefits: "the washing away of the guilt of original sin . . . we enter into covenant with God . . . we are admitted into the church . . . we who were by nature children of wrath are made the children of God . . . we are heirs of the kingdom of heaven" (Wesley, *Works X*, pp. 190-92). Wesley affirmed that the action of God and the faith of the Church in baptism could overcome original sin and bestow new life. Although Christians can fall away from baptismal grace, the ritual has a sacramental efficacy that can initiate the Spirit-filled life.

Following this tradition, the Baptismal Covenant, as found in the services in both *The United Methodist Hymnal* and *The United Methodist Book of Worship*, initiates persons into the Church, incorporates people into God's mighty acts of salvation, and gives us new birth through water and the Spirit. In this covenant, individual persons and the whole congregation renounce the spiritual forces of wickedness, accept the freedom and power God gives, confess Jesus Christ as Savior, commit themselves to the Church, profess the Christian faith, and are saved through water and the Spirit.

A number of pastors and congregations, however, have found that the services of the Baptismal Covenant in our hymnal are too complex and difficult to use. Some have discovered the services are too long, with too many options, reflecting a theology of baptism at odds with personal and congregational beliefs. While most pastors and congregations want to use our official services, many have found these baptismal liturgies the most troublesome services in our hymnal. What can be done?

The United Methodist Book of Worship is one response to these concerns. While the book of worship cannot resolve all the identified problem areas, it does attempt to clarify, supplement, and offer help in celebrating these baptismal services in your congregation. Another response is our denomination's ongoing work on a foundational document on baptism. The next generation of United Methodist liturgical reformers will probably revise all of these baptismal liturgies. Until then, however, how can you celebrate the Baptismal Covenant in your congregation?

The United Methodist Hymnal includes the four most common congregational services of the Baptismal Covenant (a combined service, a service for children, a service for adults, and a congregational reaffirmation of the Baptismal Covenant). It was thought that the services were so clear and self-explanatory that they would teach themselves. This has proven inaccurate. *The United Methodist Book of Worship*, therefore, supplements these services in a wide variety of ways. The following commentary will concentrate on how to use the services found in the hymnal, as supplemented by the book of worship, in the best possible way.

INTRODUCTION

The Introduction to the Services of the Baptismal Covenant found in *The United Methodist Book of Worship* (81-85) is a brief summary of our current United Methodist understanding of baptism. It is one attempt to describe the meaning and practice of baptism in our tradition.

One of the major problems in celebrating the baptismal services in our United Methodist congregations is our profound lack of agreement about the theology of baptism. For example, should pastors rebaptize persons upon request? Should pastors emphasize the value of infant baptism? What is the appropriate age for confirmation? Should pastors encourage immersion versus sprinkling versus pouring? Because many pastors and congregations answer these questions in different ways and there is at present no definitive United Methodist theology of baptism, the practice of baptism varies. And while almost everyone wants final answers, there are none at the present moment.

The Introduction is one place for your congregation to begin talking about baptism. The paragraphs deal with the time and place of baptism, recognition of persons baptized in other churches, the modes of baptism, the relationship of baptism to the whole of the Christian life, the relationship of baptism to the other rites of the Church, the age for baptism, the need for baptismal training, the responsibilities of the congregation for the baptized, and other particular issues related to baptism. Your congregation may reprint these pages, along with The Baptismal Covenant I, and study them together. When you come to agreement about these pages, planning for baptism in your congregation will be easier. To assist you in your work, you may also use Hoyt Hickman's *Workbook on Communion and Baptism* and chapter 6, "Services of the Baptismal Covenant" in *The Worship Resources of The United Methodist Hymnal* (see Additional Resources).

THE BAPTISMAL COVENANT I

This is the first and primary service of the Baptismal Covenant. It provides a combined service for the five primary rites related to baptism: Holy Baptism, Confirmation, Reaffirmation of Faith, Reception into The United Methodist Church, and Reception into a Local Congregation. While often thought of as separate services, all of these rituals are related to the Baptismal Covenant and need to be understood as parts of a whole.

Baptismal Covenant I is found in *The United Methodist Hymnal*, pages 33-39, and with expanded rubrics in *The United Methodist Book of Worship*, pages 86-94. This service may be used for any one of the five baptismal rites listed above, or any combination of these rites that may be called for on a given occasion. Because Baptismal Covenant I is the service most often used and is the basis of every other service of the Baptismal Covenant in our hymnal and book of worship, once you know this service well, every other service of the Baptismal Covenant will quickly become more understandable and usable.

To make it easier to determine which parts of Baptismal Covenant I to use on any given occasion, it is first of all necessary to see that the service itself has sixteen distinctive units. Each unit is part of a greater whole of the Baptismal Covenant. These parts of the service are:

1. Introduction to Baptism
2. Introduction to Confirmation and Reaffirmation
3. Presentation of Candidates
4. Renunciation of Sin and Profession of Faith
5. Parents' and Sponsors' Vow to Nurture the Child
6. Vows by Youth or Adult Candidates
7. Vows by Sponsors of Youth or Adult Candidates
8. Congregation's Vows
9. The Apostles' Creed
10. Thanksgiving over the Water
11. Baptism with Laying On of Hands

12. Confirmation or Reaffirmation of Faith
13. Congregational Reaffirmation of the Baptismal Covenant
14. Reception into The United Methodist Church
15. Reception into the Local Congregation
16. Commendation and Welcome

This list is also provided in the Introduction to the baptismal services in *The United Methodist Book of Worship* and the worksheet at the end of this chapter.

This list does seem to be long, complex, and occasionally repetitive. Yet, each one of these actions serves a particular function and reflects a specific Wesleyan theological perspective. It is now up to your congregation, and the particular occasion, to determine which of these actions you will use in worship.

The United Methodist Book of Worship provides a few examples of how to use this list. For example:

"If only persons who can take the vows for themselves are being baptized and received into the Church, and there are no confirmations or reaffirmations of faith, sections 5, 12, and 13 are omitted. Section 7 is used only if there are sponsors." In other words, if one adult wants to be baptized and received into the Church, you would use everything except the vows by parents, the words of confirmation, the congregational vows of reaffirmation, and only use vows by sponsors (a fellowship friend or host family) if your congregation uses sponsors.

"If there are only confirmation and no baptisms, sections 5 and 11 are omitted. Section 7 is used only if there are sponsors. Section 10 is used only if water is to be used, Section 13 is optional." Or, in plain English, if a youth baptized as a child wishes to join your congregation through confirmation, you would use everything except the parents' vows to nurture the youth, the baptism. You may or may not include vows by sponsors (if you use such in your congregation), Thanksgiving over the Water, and the Congregational Reaffirmation of the Baptismal Covenant.

The book of worship also provides other examples, but they are only examples and are not exhaustive of each possibility. Every pastor knows that each situation involving the Baptismal Covenant is different. Gone are the days when babies of a two-parent Christian family are the only persons baptized. While, therefore, the Baptismal Covenant services allow flexibility for almost every occasion, each pastor must review the full service in advance, make the necessary decisions, and then carefully lead the congregation through the service.

When planning to use a service of the Baptismal Covenant in your congregation, until this service becomes known well by your congregation (which will happen), it is important to review the list of sixteen parts and choose which ones you will use for a particular situation. Then mark those numbers in your hymnal or book of worship. And finally, tell the congregation that your Baptismal Covenant service will be used, such as by putting an announcement in your worship bulletin:

THE BAPTISMAL COVENANT FOR NAME OF ADULT
The Baptismal Covenant I, page 33, all except 5, 12, 13

The worksheet on page 61 will provide you with a model to use as you plan for your congregation.

THE BAPTISMAL COVENANT II

"If there are no confirmations or reaffirmations of faith or receptions by transfer, and if the only persons being baptized are (1) children who cannot take their own vows or (2) youth or adults who have not reached the developmental stage of making decisions for themselves," The Baptismal Covenant II is the service you should use.

This is the full and complete service of baptism for children. While some pastors have complained that the service is too long, it is only about two minutes longer than the shorter services now found in the book of worship. This additional length is due entirely to the inclusion of the Apostles' Creed and the Thanksgiving over the Water.

THE BAPTISMAL COVENANT II-A/
THE BAPTISMAL COVENANT II-B

With the publication of *The United Methodist Hymnal*, some congregations found that the full text of The Baptismal Covenant II for children was too long. As a result, many pastors asked for A Brief Order of Holy Baptism for Children and Others Unable to Answer for Themselves. In response, *The United Methodist Book of Worship* provides two brief orders for the baptism of children. For both services, only the pastor needs a copy of the service, found only in *The United Methodist Book of Worship*.

The Baptismal Covenant II-A, given its awkward name so as not to change the numbers of the subsequent rituals of the Baptismal Covenant in the hymnal and the book of worship, is a contemporary text based on The Baptismal Covenant II. The Introduction and Presentation may be led either from the given text in the book of worship (p. 100) or extempore. The Renunciation of Sin and Profession of Faith compresses the basic questions of faith found in The Baptismal Covenant I. There is no corporate Affirmation of Faith, and the Thanksgiving over the Water has been shortened. The congregational commendation does not include a formal prayer, although your congregation may participate by turning to item 16 in the hymnal (p. 38 or 43).

The Baptismal Covenant II-B is from the rituals of the former Methodist and former Evangelical United Brethren churches, and it uses more traditional language. The Baptismal Covenant II-B includes the option of a Congregational Pledge (use one of the two pledges provided) in response to the baptism. These two pledges are also found in *The United Methodist Hymnal,* and your congregation will need to turn to *UMH* 44 to participate in the service.

THE BAPTISMAL COVENANT III

This service, written during the 1988 General Conference, uses traditional texts from the rituals of the former Methodist and former Evangelical United Brethren churches for use with youth and adults. The service includes a ritual for Holy Baptism, Confirmation, Reaffirmation of Faith, Reception into The United Methodist Church, and Reception into a Local Congregation. While preserving some traditional prayers and phrases, the service nevertheless follows the basic pattern established in The Baptismal Covenant I.

This service is best used when youth or adults only are either being baptized and confirmed or simply being confirmed and received into the Church. Your congregation may follow along in their hymnals, while the pastor uses the service from the book of worship (which provides more extensive rubrics and thus makes the service easier for a leader to preside).

If adults and youth are to be baptized, confirmed, and received into your congregation, use the whole service. Because in many situations some youth and adults will need to be baptized and others not, pastors may need to mark in their hymnal or book of worship which youth and adults will be asked each question.

If only youth are being confirmed, but no one needs baptism, leave out the Prayer for Those to be Baptized and the Baptism, but use the rest of the service.

THE BAPTISMAL COVENANT IV

The Congregational Reaffirmation of the Baptismal Covenant (*UMBOW* 111-14 and *UMH* 50) is one of our most powerful worship and evangelistic experiences. In this service, used only when no persons are to be baptized, confirmed, or received into the Church, your whole congregation renounces evil, accepts freedom, confesses Christ, and affirms the faith. Then with symbolic liturgical acts (such as the water being lifted for all to see, water being sprinkled toward the people, or persons coming forward to touch the water to their head, face, or heart), the people remember that they have been baptized and are thankful. This is similar to Holy Communion in that the liturgical action wholly involves the congregation—the action of taking and receiving is theirs.

The particular days most appropriate for this service are New Year's Eve or New Year's Day (instead of the Wesleyan Covenant Renewal Service), at The Baptism of the Lord (the First Sunday After the Epiphany), at The Easter Vigil, on All Saints Day, or at your congregation's anniversary or homecoming.

The congregation may follow along in their hymnals, while the pastor uses the service from the book of worship (which provides more extensive rubrics and thus makes the service easier for a leader to preside).

MUSIC AND THE BAPTISMAL COVENANT

In *The United Methodist Hymnal* we notice the apparent lack of appropriate music for baptisms. There are only seven hymns in the section on baptism. *The United Methodist Book of Worship* has responded to this concern by providing a more comprehensive list of hymns that are appropriate at baptisms (*UMBOW* 84-85). They are placed in the categories of General (appropriate for all age levels), For Children, For Youth, and For Adults or Reaffirmation.

In addition, the *Book of Worship* includes three new pieces of music for baptism (*UMBOW* 173-75). Each of these may be sung by the whole congregation or by a choir or solo voice. They are brief, clear, and have excellent tunes. Singing is one of the best ways your congregation may participate in the Baptismal Covenant. Always use as much music as possible.

PASTORAL SUGGESTIONS

The liturgical leadership of the Baptismal Covenant demands particular attention by your pastor. In addition to the suggestions given in *The United Methodist Book of Worship* for each of the services, here are some other suggestions to enrich your practice of baptism:

1. Baptize particularly on the days of The Baptism of the Lord, at the Easter Vigil, throughout The Great Fifty Days of Easter, on Pentecost, and on All Saints Day.

2. Nonverbally walk through the whole service to be sure that every action corresponds to the text spoken.

3. Keep the baptismal font or pool continually in view. The font/pool should also be visible on Sundays without baptisms.

4. Encourage the parents, sponsors, or a leader of the congregation to present or introduce a child, youth, or adult to your congregation in their own words. This is especially valuable when someone in your congregation has been the spiritual guide of the candidate.

5. Let the water be clearly visible. Pour the water from a clear glass pitcher into the font or pool.

6. Thoroughly wet the candidates by dipping infants or by immersion or pouring. Do not be afraid of using lots of water.

7. If you use much water, provide towels for the candidates and leaders.

8. Enable the congregation to watch the whole action. Ask parents, sponsors, and family members to stand to the side of the pastor or behind the pastor, facing the congregation.

It is hard to underestimate the power of the sign action of a baptism to demonstrate the basic Christian dynamic of hearing and responding to God's call of grace and redemption. When an infant or a child is baptized, the congregation remembers God's love. When a young person makes the first public reaffirmation of faith (confirmation), the people remember that responses are required. And when an adult yields to God's summons and is baptized, the congregation recalls that God's grace works in mysterious and powerful ways.

For additional help, see *The Worship Resources of The United Methodist Hymnal* in Additional Resources.

BAPTISM PLANNING SHEET

Name(s): _____.

Date: _____

Hymns and Service Music: *UMBOW* 84-85, 173-75

_____

_____

Signing with cross new clothing baptismal candle certificate

1. Introduction to Baptism
2. Introduction to Confirmation and Reaffirmation
3. Presentation of Candidates
4. Renunciation of Sin and Profession of Faith
5. Parents' and Sponsors' Vow to Nurture the Child
6. Vows by Youth or Adult Candidates
7. Vows by Sponsors of Youth or Adult Candidates
8. Congregation's Vows
9. The Apostles' Creed
10. Thanksgiving over the Water
11. Baptism with Laying On of Hands
12. Confirmation or Reaffirmation of Faith
13. Congregational Reaffirmation of the Baptismal Covenant
14. Reception into The United Methodist Church
15. Reception into the Local Congregation
16. Commendation and Welcome

8. WEDDINGS

Christian weddings are for couples who wish to solemnize their marriage in a service of Christian worship. The services in *The United Methodist Book of Worship* and *The United Methodist Hymnal* have a pattern parallel to the Sunday service, including the proclamation of the Word and the option of Holy Communion. "Christian marriage is proclaimed as a sacred covenant . . . and everything about the service is designed to witness that this is a Christian marriage."

The pastor, in consultation with the couple, is responsible for weddings in your congregation.

> The decision to perform the ceremony is the right and responsibility of the pastor, in accordance with the laws of the state and The United Methodist Church. All plans should be approved by the pastor. The pastor's due counsel with the parties involved is required by *The Book of Discipline* prior to marriage and should include, in addition to premarital counseling, discussing and planning the service with them and informing them of policies or guidelines established by the congregation on such matters as decorations, photography, and audio or video recording. Any leadership roles taken by other clergy should be at the invitation of the pastor of the church where the service is held. The organist or person in charge of the music should be consulted and work with the couple in all decisions on music selection.

To support your congregation in this ministry, *The United Methodist Book of Worship* includes an extensive set of worship services and acts of worship for pastors and couples for weddings. While *The United Methodist Hymnal* includes a congregational Service of Christian Marriage (*UMH* 864-869), the book of worship supplements this service in a wide variety of ways. In your congregation you will discover occasions for using every one of the following services and prayers found in the *Book of Worship*.

A Service of Christian Marriage I
A Service of Christian Marriage II (Traditional Methodist and E.U.B.)

A Service for the Recognition or the Blessing of a Civil Marriage
An Order for the Reaffirmation of the Marriage Covenant
Marriage Anniversary Prayers

PLANNING A CHRISTIAN WEDDING

Weddings require planning by the pastor, musician, other worship leaders in your congregation, and particularly the couple to be married. The following suggestions guide you through the essential elements of planning a marriage.

Your congregation should have a policy regarding marriage services. If your congregation does not have a set of guidelines, now is an excellent time to create such a policy. This policy should be clear about issues such as scheduling the church facilities, how long the party may remain on the premises, payments due, and the use of outside vendors, such as florists. Such a policy, however, should also retain some flexibility.

While the essential congregational acts of worship are included in the Service of Christian Marriage found in the hymnal, and the congregation may follow the service using only the hymnal, many couples desire a printed worship bulletin. Such a bulletin may give the names of all the participants, the hymn numbers, the Scripture texts, and the page of the service in the hymnal. The pastor or other leaders may then lead the service from the book of worship.

In addition to the pastoral suggestions in the book of worship, the following are the necessary decisions that must be made when a couple comes to plan their wedding. The couple and worship leaders may answer these questions on the worksheet at the end of this chapter.

1. Determine the place, time, and pastor. The place and time will affect the service in dramatic ways, and is the first and most important decision. A Service of Christian Marriage should be held in the church at a time when members of the congregation can be present. Because it is the sacred space of one's own congregation, where the couple, or at least one partner, may have worshiped and marked passages of Christian life, it is wholesome to have the wedding in the sanctuary or chapel, except in circumstances when the couple insist on having it elsewhere.

Choose a time and place that best meet the desires and schedules of the majority of family, friends, congregation, and pastor. Allow enough time for pre-marriage counseling, and also set a future date for at least one session of post-wedding counseling.

Finally, decide which pastor or pastors will participate in the service. Sometimes the choice of a pastor takes priority over the choice of a church, but at other times a couple may choose the church first and then meet the pastor. If a couple desires an outside pastor to participate at the wedding, courtesy demands that the current pastor invite the outside pastor, and that the current pastor be given primary leadership.

2. Decide Who Will Participate. The pastor and the church musician are generally the primary leaders in the service. They are in charge of planning and leading the church service. In addition to these leaders, at the request of the couple and upon invitation of the pastor in charge, other pastors and musicians often participate in specific ways.

"Any children of the man or the woman, other family, and friends may take a variety of roles in the service, depending on their ages and abilities. They may, for example, be members of the wedding party, participate in the Response of the Families and People, read scripture lessons, sing or play instrumental music, or make a witness in their own words." The book of worship provides several ways for the children and friends to participate, for example by reading Scripture, by promising to support the couple, and leading in prayer.

"Those present are understood to be an active congregation rather than simply passive witnesses. They give their blessing to the couple and to the marriage, and they join in prayer and praise." Plan the service in a way that your whole congregation may participate fully and actively, for example by singing hymns and blessing the couple.

Determine who will present the wife and/or husband to the congregation. While it is traditional for a father to present his daughter for marriage, many alternatives are now becoming popular. For example, a child from a previous marriage may present the couple.

Also alert your worship committee, custodians, or others if they are needed to arrange the sanctuary, greet the family, or clean up the sanctuary. Be sure that the doors will be unlocked and the temperature moderate.

3. Prepare the Worship Setting. White dominates the color of the vestments of the pastor and the paraments of your sanctuary. You may also use a paschal (Easter) candle. Cautiously use a unity candle (one central candle with two side candles) in a wedding. A unity candle tends to detract from the central symbolic acts of giving and receiving vows and rings, so the book of worship provides suggestions on how to use the unity candle.

4. Rings or Other Symbols. The giving and receiving of rings is always central to the wedding ceremony. Determine whether you will use one or two rings. Choose who will carry the rings in the ceremony, a child or other member of the wedding party. Other symbols may also be exchanged, such as a piece of family jewelry.

5. Exchange of Vows. A Service of Christian Marriage in the hymnal and A Service of Christian Marriage II in the book of worship include only one Exchange of Vows ("I, NAME, take you, NAME . . . "). A Service of Christian Marriage I in the book of worship, however, includes three sets of vows from which you may choose. Determine which set of vows, or variation thereof, you will use. Couples are also free to create their own marriage vows.

7. Choose Scripture. Choosing Scripture is a decision that must be made for each service to fit the particular situation. While many people pick a favorite or traditional text quickly, give serious attention to the most appropriate texts for this occasion. Although the book of worship encourages three lessons and a psalm, you may choose more or fewer lessons. *The United Methodist Book of Worship* (119) has an exhaustive list of Scripture lessons from which to choose. You may wish to copy this list and provide it to family and friends.

8. Select Hymns. Hymns and other musical acts of worship are appropriate during a Christian wedding. See the wedding hymns in *The United Methodist Hymnal* (642-47), those listed under "Weddings" (953), and others listed in the service in *The United Methodist Book of Worship* (116, 119, 127). Hymns are the primary way many people in your congregation will participate in this service, and this opportunity for ministry should not be given to another. The organist or person in charge of the music should be consulted and work with the family in all decisions on music selection. Like Scripture, choosing hymns is among the most important decisions to make. While many persons name favorite or traditional hymns, encourage them to look at hymns that would be most appropriate for this particular service. You may even wish to note in a hymnal the hymns most appropriate to a marriage service.

9. Holy Communion. Increasingly, Holy Communion is becoming a part of weddings. The book of worship provides a Prayer of Great Thanksgiving for Holy Communion for weddings (*UMBOW* 124-26). If you decide to celebrate Holy Communion, answer at least the following questions: Recognizing that not only the husband and the wife receive Communion, but the whole congregation is invited to receive as well, will the couple or family help serve the holy meal? Will everyone receive? Because persons from other churches and other religions may be present, be clear in the pastoral invitation who may receive. Please be aware that there should be no pressure that would embarrass those who for whatever reason do not choose to receive Communion. For additional help with this ministry, see *Your Ministry of Planning a Christian Wedding* in Additional Resources.

SERVICE OF CHRISTIAN MARRIAGE I

A Service of Christian Marriage I is found in *UMH* 864-69 and with additional resources and suggestions in *UMBOW* 115-27. This service of Christian worship is suitable for the marriage services of all Christians. It is a full service of Word and Table and includes your congregation in many ways. Its contemporary language makes this service very popular.

SERVICE OF CHRISTIAN MARRIAGE II
(TRADITIONAL METHODIST AND E.U.B.)

The United Methodist Book of Worship (128-33) includes a traditional text for marriage from the services of the former denominations of our Church. The service is a very free adaption of the service of Holy Matrimony in *The Book of Common Prayer* of the Church of England, which John Wesley sent to the American Methodists in 1784. This service was not included in *The United Methodist Hymnal* because the service requires no congregational participation other than the Lord's Prayer. It has, however, been in our official rituals for two hundred years, was requested for inclusion by many United Methodists, and thus is included in our new book of worship. Because this service is less specific about the Christian commitment of the couple, many have found it to be more usable for the marriage of persons not related to a local congregation.

The only major changes to this traditional text are that two charges by the pastor are provided (one from the former Methodist *The United Methodist Book of Worship*, and the other from the former E.U.B. *Book of Ritual*), the man as well as the woman may be presented by a member of the family, and rubrics are given for the possible inclusion of a unity candle and Holy Communion.

RECOGNITION/BLESSING OF A MARRIAGE

Many couples are married in congregations other than the one in which they will live and work; in our increasingly secular culture, couples are married outside the Church and by persons other than pastors of local congregations. This order (in *UMBOW* 133-35) allows the congregation to recognize and bless a couple married in another place or outside the Church. It enables the couple to declare their covenant in front of their home congregation and to have their own congregation and pastor bless their marriage. This service may be used on a Sunday morning following a service of the Word, or more often, at a special service of recognition or blessing. Your congregation will be able to follow the service better if it is printed in a worship bulletin.

REAFFIRMATION OF THE MARRIAGE COVENANT

On particular occasions in the marriage of any couple, there may come a time to reaffirm the marriage covenant. It may come after many years of wedded bliss, or after a period of estrangement followed by reconciliation. At these and many other occasions, your congregation may support the marriage of a couple by a special order or service. This service (in *UMBOW* 135-38), may be used on a Sunday morning following a service of the Word, or more often, at a special service of reaffirmation by one or more couples. The congregation will be able to follow the service better if it is printed in a worship bulletin. Three items will make this a superior service in your congregation.

1. Let the couple or couples themselves plan the service. Have them write or rewrite the Greeting, Reaffirmation of the Marriage Covenant, Congregational Response, and Blessing of the Marriage. The more personal the liturgy, the more powerful the service.

2. Involve as many family members as possible in the service. Parents, siblings, children, and other family and friends have all benefited from this marriage. Let them participate in the service and affirm the marriage. To assist this affirmation, you may choose to let individuals voice brief thanksgivings for the marriage of the couple.

3. Involve everyone directly in Holy Communion. Celebrate the holy meal using the Prayer of Great Thanksgiving for a Christian Marriage (*UMBOW* 124-26), and then let the couple(s) serve the congregation.

MARRIAGE ANNIVERSARY PRAYERS

The book of worship contains two marriage anniversary prayers (*UMBOW* 138). Either one or both of these may be integrated into any regular worship service of your congregation, or they may be used in a special service celebrating a marriage anniversary (such as a marriage reaffirmation). The first prayer is said by a pastor, while the second prayer is said by the couple.

WEDDING CHECKLIST

Names: _____

Place: _____

Wedding Date and Time: _____

Rehearsal Date and Time: _____

1. State marriage license _____
2. Church wedding information leaflet/guidelines _____
3. Wedding conferences with pastor(s) _____
4. Wedding conferences with organist/music director _____
5. Wedding conferences with other church personnel _____
6. Persons participating in the wedding:

    bridal party _____

    groom's party _____

    presenter(s) _____

    other attendants _____

    soloists _____

    instrumentalists _____

    choir _____

    Scripture readers _____

    children of previous marriages _____

    other participants _____

7. Music:

    processional (see *UMBOW* 116) _____

    recessional (see *UMBOW* 127) _____

    hymns (see *UMBOW* 119) _____

    solo/choral _____

    instrumental _____

8. ring or other symbol _____
9. unity candle _____
10. vows (see *UMBOW* 120, 121, 130) _____

9. FUNERALS

A Christian funeral is a significant moment of passage in the Christian community. Faced with the reality of death, your community gathers together to worship. Acknowledging grief and loss, the people remember the person who has died and then proclaim the good news: Jesus Christ triumphs over death. By our acknowledging both hurt and hope, God grants comfort and new life.

To support your congregation in this ministry, *The United Methodist Book of Worship* includes an extensive set of worship services and acts of worship for pastors, leaders of worship, and families at the time of death. While *The United Methodist Hymnal* includes the congregational Service of Death and Resurrection (*UMH* 870-75), the book of worship supplements this service in a wide variety of ways. In your congregation you will discover occasions for using almost every service and prayer found in the book of worship.

The United Methodist Book of Worship includes the following resources for your use:

A Service of Death and Resurrection
   An Order for Holy Communion
   A Service of Committal

Additional Resources for Services of Death and Resurrection
   For General Use
   At the Service for a Child
   An Untimely or Tragic Death
   At the Service for a Person Who Did Not Profess the Christian Faith
   Ministry with the Dying
   Ministry Immediately Following Death
   A Family Hour or Wake
   A Service of Death and Resurrection for a Stillborn Child

A SERVICE OF DEATH AND RESURRECTION

A Service of Death and Resurrection is found in *UMH* 870-75 and with additional resources and suggestions in *UMBOW* 139-51. This service of Christian worship is suitable for funerals and memorial services for all Christians. The title of this service has proven troublesome to some United Methodists. The introduction in the book of worship states:

> Use of the term "Service of Death and Resurrection" is not intended to discourage use of the more familiar terms "funeral," "burial of the dead," or "memorial service." "Funeral" is appropriate for a service with the body of the deceased present. "Burial of the dead" is appropriate for a service where the remains of the deceased are buried. "Memorial service" is appropriate where the body of the deceased is not present. "Service of Death and Resurrection" was selected as being appropriate to any of the wide variety of situations in which this service might be used. It expresses clearly the twofold nature of what is done: the facts of death and bereavement are honestly faced, and the gospel of resurrection is celebrated in the context of God's Baptismal Covenant with us in Christ."

In summary, you may name the service a funeral, a memorial service, burial of the dead, or a service of death and resurrection.

This service requires planning by the pastor, musician, and other worship leaders in your congregation, as well as the family and friends of the deceased. In some cases, persons dying may also participate in the planning of their own funerals, for example during pastoral care with the terminally ill. In most instances, however, funeral planning occurs in the days and hours between the death of an individual and the service itself. The following suggestions will help guide you through the essential elements of planning a funeral.

If your congregation doesn't have a set of guidelines for funerals, now is an excellent time to create such a policy. The policy should be clear about issues such as scheduling the church facilities, memorials, and the use of outside vendors, such as florists. These policies, however, should retain some flexibility. In addition, encourage the individuals in your congregation, through study and training, to prepare for their own funerals. Such pre-planning is a wonderful spiritual journey that will enrich each participant and make the planning of a service much easier.

In most cases, it is not necessary to print a worship bulletin for the service. All the essential congregational acts of worship are included in the service found in the hymnal, and the congregation may follow the service using only the hymnal. The pastor or other leaders may lead the service from the book of worship, and announce the hymns and Scripture texts at the appropriate time.

In addition to all the pastoral suggestions in the book of worship, the following decisions will be made when death has occurred. You may answer these questions on the worksheet at the end of this chapter.

1. Determine the place and time. The Service of Death and Resurrection "should be held in the church if at all possible, and at a time when members of the congregation can be present." Because the sacred space of one's own congregation, where the deceased may have worshiped and marked passages of Christian life, such as baptism and marriage, is so important, have the funeral there except in rare circumstances. Choose a time and place that best meet the desires and schedules of the majority of family, friends, congregation, pastor, and funeral home.

2. Decide who will participate. The pastor and church musician are the primary participants in the service. They must be in charge of planning and leading the service. In addition to these leaders, at the request of family and friends, and upon invitation of the pastor in charge, other pastors and musicians may participate in specific ways.

■ Even more important, "members of the deceased's family, friends, and members of the congregation are encouraged strongly to share in conducting the service." These persons may read Scripture, lead prayer, and participate in the naming (when the life and death of the deceased is gathered up by the reading of an obituary, a memorial, or other appropriate statement) and witnessing (short thanksgivings when persons "briefly voice their thankfulness to God for the grace they have received in the life of the deceased and their Christian faith and joy"). In your congregation, if such witness and naming have not been typical, you may wish to alert certain individuals in advance and enable them to prepare to speak.

■ Alert your worship committee, custodians, or others if they are needed to arrange the sanctuary, greet the family, or clean up the sanctuary. Be sure that the doors will be unlocked and the temperature moderate.

■ Finally, choose pallbearers and ushers to perform their necessary roles in the service. Typically, six pallbearers are enough. For help with this ministry, see *Your Ministry of Ushering and Greeting* in Additional Resources.

3. Memorials and flowers. Will you encourage memorial gifts for the church, a charity, or another institution? Make a decision and let the community know through obituaries and worship bulletins. Flowers, signs of honor and respect, may either enhance or detract from the service. Determine if you must limit the number of flowers, especially in the sanctuary, and let the funeral home know in advance.

4. Pall, flag, or flowers on the casket. Will a pall (a large cloth with border or appliqué that completely covers a casket), a national flag, or a spray of flowers cover the casket? The pall serves as a sign of unity among all the members of your congregation, while the flag is a sign of military service to one's country. Choose which one to use.

5. Fraternal, civic, or military rites. Many fraternal, civic, and military organizations encourage a last ritual moment before interment. "If the family requests that there be military, fraternal, or other rites in addition to the Service of Death and Resurrection, the pastor should plan carefully the sequence and interrelationship of these services so that the service is not interrupted with other rites, and so that its integrity is supported and not compromised."

6. Prepare the worship setting. White or green dominates the color of the vestments of the pastor, the paraments of your sanctuary, and pall. You may also use a paschal (Easter) candle. In addition to these basic signs, a family or personal Bible, a picture of the deceased, or a valued object may be used in a secondary way.

7. Place of the casket, coffin, or urn. "The coffin remains closed throughout the service and thereafter." This traditional act should be confirmed with the family. Placing the coffin before the congregation acknowledges the reality of death without undue attention to the body. Traditionally, the head of the coffin is away from the altar/table, except in the case of clergy, when the head is toward the altar/table. An urn may be set in a place easily seen by the congregation.

8. Choose prayers and creeds. Congregational participation is crucial in a Service of Death and Resurrection. Determine which prayers to use and print them in the service. Use the creeds found in *The United Methodist Hymnal* (880-89, esp. 880, 883, and 887).

9. Choose Scripture. Choosing Scripture is a decision that must be made for each service to fit the particular situation. While many people pick a favorite or traditional text quickly, give serious attention to the most appropriate texts for this occasion. Although the book of worship encourages three lessons and a psalm, you may choose more or fewer lessons. *The United Methodist Book of Worship* (144-48, 159, 162, 164, 166) has exhaustive lists of Scripture lessons from which to choose. You may wish to copy these lists and provide them to family and friends.

10. Select hymns. The book of worship and the hymnal clearly prefer congregational singing to the use of solos and choir anthems for a Service of Death and Resurrection. Hymns are the primary way many people in the congregation will participate in this service, and this opportunity for ministry should not be given to another. "The organist or person in charge of the music should be consulted and work with the family in all decisions on music selection."

Like Scripture, choosing hymns is among the most important decisions you will make. While many persons name favorite or traditional hymns, encourage persons to look at the hymns that would be most appropriate for this particular service. You may even wish to note in one copy of the hymnal the hymns most appropriate to a Service of Death and Resurrection. (An exhaustive list of hymns is found in *UMBOW* 160-61, 163, 164, 166.)

11. Holy Communion. Increasingly, Holy Communion is becoming a part of funerals and memorial services. The book of worship provides a Prayer of Great Thanksgiving for Holy Communion for memorial services and funerals (*UMBOW* 152-54). If you decide to celebrate Holy Communion, answer at least the following questions: Will the family help serve the holy meal? Will everyone receive? Knowing that persons from other churches and other faiths will be present, be clear in the pastoral invitation who may receive. There should be no pressure that would embarrass those who for whatever reason do not choose to receive Communion.

12. Committal. The committal service is not found in *The United Methodist Hymnal* because the congregation cannot be expected to carry hymnals to the graveside, but it is found in the book of worship (*UMBOW* 155-57). The committal may take place immediately following the funeral, or it may be a separate service at another time and place.

Two major decisions may face you as you plan the committal. First, this is the place where fraternal, civic, or military rites are most often used. As noted before, the pastor must determine ahead of time the appropriate sequence of rites. For example, such orders and honors may occur immediately before the committal, which preserves the integrity of the Christian service and allows the last word to be the Word of God. Yet, certain acts—such as the giving of the flag, rifle volleys, and the playing of "Taps"—may best follow the committal. Second, persons increasingly are asking for a simple graveside service rather than a full service in a sanctuary or funeral home. In this case, the committal service will need to be supplemented by additional readings from Scripture, a short sermon, and a time for naming and witness. Each of these twelve steps of planning a funeral can be noted on the worksheet at the end of this chapter.

ADDITIONAL RESOURCES FOR SERVICES OF DEATH AND RESURRECTION

The United Methodist Book of Worship adds a number of worship resources that may be added to the basic Service of Death and Resurrection. Because many funerals and memorial services deal with a particular kind of death, and planning time is often limited, these resources will likely become a basic part of your congregation's worship repertoire.

For general use, the book of worship provides additional Words of Grace, opening Sentences, Prayers, Scripture Readings, and Suggested Hymns (*UMBOW* 158-61). Any of these could be used in almost any service. The Scripture Readings are the most common alternative readings (with the recommended readings already provided in the Service of Death and Resurrection itself). The Suggested Hymns are an exhaustive list of the appropriate hymns from the hymnal. You may wish to make a copy of both the Scripture Readings and the Suggested Hymns to share with a dying person, family, or friends, to involve them in the planning process.

At the Service for a Child and For an Untimely or Tragic Death (*UMBOW* 161-64), the book of worship suggests additional Words of Grace, opening Sentences, Prayers, Scripture Readings, and Suggested Hymns. These services are obviously among the most difficult for any congregation, and the book of worship provides a starting place for your planning.

One of the most difficult services to conduct in the book of worship is At the Service for a Person Who Did Not Profess the Christian Faith (*UMBOW* 165-66). What does one say in a funeral when the deceased was an active believer of another religion, or chose not to profess the Christian faith? The Service of Death and Resurrection is clearly Christian and assumes that the deceased participates in the Christian affirmation of life beyond death. The resources in this section help you decide what to say when that is not the case. The Words of Grace, Opening Sentences, Prayers, Scripture Readings, and Suggested Hymns all provide you with a starting place that will not violate the faith of the deceased, the family and friends of the deceased, and your own Christian community.

ADDITIONAL MINISTRIES AND SERVICES

At the time of a death, there are additional ministries that should be a part of the ongoing worship life of your congregation. The pastor, especially, must be prepared and able to minister to a dying person, family, and friends in a variety of ways as an expression of your congregation's love.

Ministry with the Dying (UMBOW 166) provides prayer resources for use with the dying person either soon or immediately before death. These prayers, found for the first time in a United Methodist book of worship, are most similar to the Roman Catholic sacrament of Extreme Unction. These resources are not exhaustive, but provide you with a starting point as you pray with the dying.

Immediately after a person has died, Ministry Immediately Following Death (UMBOW 167) is one way to care for the family and friends of the deceased. Again, these resources are not exhaustive but suggestive of how you might begin to pray with the family and friends at this time.

A Family Hour or Wake (UMBOW 168-69) is a brief pattern of worship that may be held with family and friends before the Service of Death and Resurrection. It comes out of African-American worship traditions in our denomination. The most common location for this service will be at the home of a family member, the church, or the funeral home on the day or night before the full service. It is primarily a time for the people to gather to express their thoughts and emotions in a more informal way. This is not the time for a sermon or extended liturgy, but for family and friends to "voice their thankfulness to God for the grace they have received in the life of the deceased and their Christian faith and joy."

A Service of Death and Resurrection for a Stillborn Child (UMBOW 170-71), because of the tragedy and prematurity of the situation, is the most distinctive of all the resources in this section, and thus is a complete service of worship. The most difficult aspect of this service is the pastoral support given to the mother or couple and the family and friends, particularly as it is expressed through the sermon. This is no time for simple answers or abstract theological debate. Deal directly with the family and their pain and grief, and enable the congregation to express its love and concern.

Finally, following death, "reentry into the community by the chief mourners following the service takes time and can be facilitated by the supportive ministry of the Church." Ministry to a family does not end at the committal. It is sometimes valuable for your pastor to bring Communion to the family, perhaps at the first visit following the service. "Recurring memorial acts and services are occasions both of healing and of celebration. Mourners are especially open to supportive ministries on such occasions as Christmas, holidays, birthdays, and anniversaries of marriage or of death. Celebration of All Saints (see UMBOW 413-15) and other annual memorial services can also be particularly helpful (see

UMBOW 548)." Your congregation will benefit if it keeps an annual calendar noting the date of death of your members, and then remembering these people in worship on the anniversary of their death.

For further assistance, see *Your Ministry of Planning a Christian Funeral* in the Additional Resources.

FUNERAL CHECKLIST

Name: _____

Funeral Date and Time: _____

Funeral Location: Church _____ Funeral Home: _____

Visitation: Place: _____ Time: _____

Coffin Before Service: _____ closed _____ open

Interment Location: _____

Pastor(s): _____

_____

Musician(s): _____

_____

Honorarium: _____ yes _____ no

Other Participants (family, friends, members of congregation for reading of Scripture, naming, and witness): _____

_____

Pallbearers: _____

_____

Ushers: _____

_____

Visuals: white or green paraments, paschal candle

Old Testament: UMBOW 144, 145, 159

Psalm(s): 130, 23, or UMBOW 148, 159

Epistle: UMBOW 145-147, 159-160

Gospel: UMBOW 148, 160

Hymns: UMBOW 160, 161

_____

_____

Other Music: _____

Creed: UMH 880-889

Holy Communion: see UMBOW 152-154

Pall: _____ yes _____ no

Flag: _____ yes _____ no

Memorial(s): _____

Fraternal, Military, Civic Rites: _____ yes _____ no

Committal Service at Graveside: _____ yes _____ no

PART TWO:

THE CHRISTIAN YEAR CYCLE

The Christian year enables your congregation to hear the story of Jesus Christ, from the anticipation of the Messiah to his birth, manifestation, baptism, transfiguration, passion, death, resurrection, and ascension to the coming of the Holy Spirit upon the community of faith and the mighty acts of God throughout the ages. As God's story becomes incarnate in your congregation, the people begin to pattern their lives on the model of Jesus Christ. Many of the services of worship in *The United Methodist Hymnal* and *The United Methodist Book of Worship* encourage significant portions of Scripture to be read in this way.

The year rests on two cycles based on the Gospel readings. The first, yet lesser, cycle is Advent/Christmas/Epiphany. This cycle narrates the anticipation, birth, and manifestation of Jesus Christ. The greater cycle is Lent/Easter/Pentecost. This cycle tells of Christ's anticipated glory, the Resurrection, and the creation of the church.

The United Methodist Book of Worship includes four general resources to assist you in following the Christian year in your congregation.

THE CALENDAR

On one page the calendar provides an overview of the whole Christian year. It names each season, provides the correct title for the Sundays and special days found in each season, and suggests the appropriate colors for the season or day. This calendar follows the calendrical system proposed by the *Revised Common Lectionary*, and it is the calendar most often used in churches throughout the world. Although some other denominations may choose to name a season or day differently (e.g., Anglicans observe the Transfiguration on the Second Sunday in Lent), this calendar is the most ecumenical. There is no difference between the naming of seasons and days in the hymnal and the book of worship. This page may become an excellent teaching tool to instruct worship leaders and the congregation about the Christian year.

CALENDAR FOR DATING EASTER

On one page, the chart provides the dates for Ash Wednesday, Easter Day, the Day of Pentecost, and the First Sunday of Advent from 1992 to 2020. This chart is essential for long-range planning, especially when you use secular calendars that do not include sacred days.

COLORS FOR THE CHRISTIAN YEAR

Related to the Christian year, more people ask questions about liturgical colors than anything else. This page provides a brief introduction to the use of colors and the general significance of each color. Your altar guild or flower directory may use this one page more than any other in the new book of worship.

Color is an essential element of your worship. Like all the other visuals and signs in your worship environment, the color(s) used in any service of worship may either enhance or detract from the focus of the day. Colors may vary, and there are no absolute rules that must be followed in your congregation. The key criterion is appropriateness. Does the color you choose support the mystery of worship and serve the movement of the service? Do not be bound by the suggestions given; be creative and use the color that best reflects the focus of your service. For further help, see *United Methodist Altars* in Additional Resources.

REVISED COMMON LECTIONARY

A United Methodist version of the *Revised Common Lectionary* is provided in the book of worship. More pastors requested the complete lectionary than any other item for our new book of worship. This lectionary provides worship planners with the first foundation stone of worship, Scripture, in a full three-year cycle.

This lectionary, a 1992 major revision of the 1983 *Common Lectionary*, reflects significant biblical and pastoral critique of the 1983 lectionary. Although many pastors and worship planners have worship resources and aids based on the 1983 lectionary, this 1992 lectionary is significantly improved, and new resources provided by Abingdon Press and other publishers will replace previous resources. Most likely, this lectionary will last throughout the life of *The United Methodist Book of Worship*.

As the introduction in the book of worship explains, "The *Revised Common Lectionary* (1992) is a calendar and table of suggested Scripture readings for a three-year cycle of readings. The readings for each Sunday and holy day—typically one each from the Old Testament, Epistles, and

Gospels—are meant for the weekly service of worship on the Lord's Day. It provides a systematic approach to the use of Scripture in worship."

"The lectionary follows the outline of the Christian year. In it the Church celebrates the central mystery of our faith: the life, death, and resurrection of Christ Jesus. The foundation is the Lord's Day, the first day of the week, on which we recall Christ's triumph over sin and death. Each year there are two Christ-centered cycles: Advent/Christmas/ Epiphany and Lent/Easter/Pentecost. In each cycle, days of preparation (Advent and Lent) are followed by days of celebration (Christmas/ Epiphany and Easter/Pentecost)." The color system proposed in the book of worship follows and enhances the basic shape of the lectionary.

"The lectionary is a tool for voluntary use in planning and leading worship. Its widespread use by United Methodists as well as other Christians testifies to its value in helping congregations hear the whole message of Scripture." The United Methodist Church does not require that all pastors and congregations follow the lectionary. Over two-thirds of our United Methodist congregations, however, hear Scripture read in the systematic manner suggested by the lectionary. In your congregation, the pastor and laymembers may read and study these Scripture lessons prior to services of worship at home or in small study groups. Your worship services should encourage clergy and laity to read these lessons together. The use of the lectionary may encourage your congregation to become a people of the Book.

"Versification is based on the *New Revised Standard Version* of the Bible." Part of the revision of the lectionary was to check versification and determine anew where a particular lesson should begin or end. Hundreds of changes were made to reflect more accurately the meaning of a text. If you use another translation of the Bible, you may be confused about where a reading begins or ends. Not all translations break sentences or divide paragraphs in the same way. This does not mean that you must use only the NRSV for your worship, but in determining where the lessons begin and end you should have at hand the NRSV.

Finally, the lectionary in *The United Methodist Book of Worship* may be different from other lectionaries that also call themselves the *Revised Common Lectionary*. The complete lectionary (published by Abingdon Press) offers many alternative readings, especially in the Sundays After Pentecost. For a variety of theological and pastoral reasons, our new book of worship made choices from these alternatives. For example, the United Methodist version excludes readings from the Apocrypha, does not list days such as Presentation and Visitation, provides alternative psalms when the psalm suggested by the lectionary does not appear in *The United Methodist Hymnal*, and chooses to celebrate the Transfiguration on the

Last Sunday After the Epiphany. Also, in the Sundays After Pentecost, our lectionary readings for the Old Testament lesson follow a sequential series of narratives from the Old Testament rather than readings related directly to the Gospel reading for each day. The chapter "Season After Pentecost" will discuss this system more fully. If you participate in a lectionary study group with persons from other denominations, you will need to check which lessons each person will use.

10. ADVENT

Advent is a season of four weeks including four Sundays. Advent derives from the Latin adventus *that means* coming. *The season proclaims the comings of the Christ—whose birth we prepare to celebrate once again, who comes continually in Word and Spirit, and whose return in final victory we anticipate. Each year Advent calls the community of faith to prepare for each of these comings. . . . Each Sunday of Advent has its distinctive theme: Christ's coming in final victory (First Sunday), John the Baptist (Second and Third Sundays), and the events that immediately preceded the birth of Jesus Christ (Fourth Sunday).*

The United Methodist Book of Worship contains a rich variety of acts of worship and services of worship for Advent. In addition to the items found in the Advent section of the book of worship (*UMBOW* 238-68), the book of worship also contains a Prayer of Great Thanksgiving for Holy Communion for Advent (*UMBOW* 54).

The Scripture readings for Advent in the lectionary (*UMBOW* 227-28) exhibit a strong thematic unity each Sunday. The Old Testament, Psalm, and Epistle readings all revolve around the Gospel lesson of the day. The prophets, especially Isaiah, are read each year during Advent. Always look first at the Gospel reading to set the tone or theme of the day, and note how the lessons each Sunday follow the readings from the preceding week and prepare your congregation for the next week's readings.

Throughout Advent, "use the colors of purple or blue for paraments, stoles, and banners. Visuals of the season may include the use of an Advent wreath (an evergreen wreath with four purple candles and a central white Christ candle added on Christmas Eve/Day), evergreen wreaths and branches, a Chrismon tree (an evergreen tree covered with white monograms of Christ), and a Jesse tree (a tree with signs of the ancestors of Christ). Other symbols include trumpets for Isaiah, messianic rose, star of Jacob, and fleur-de-lis." The most frequently asked question about colors is why some churches use blue and others use purple. To answer briefly, purple is a sign of penance and royalty; blue is a sign of the virgin Mary (out of the thirteenth-century Sarum rite from Salisbury Cathedral in England, but never adopted by Roman Catholics).

The United Methodist Book of Worship includes the following worship resources for Advent:

Acts of Worship for Advent
Hanging of the Greens
Blessing of the Chrismon Tree
Blessing of the Advent Wreath
Lighting of the Advent Candles
An Advent Service of Lessons and Carols
Las Posadas (Service of Shelter for the Holy Family)

ACTS OF WORSHIP FOR ADVENT

The Acts of Worship for Advent include hymns and canticles, short musical responses (which may be used as brief congregational responses throughout the services), greetings, and prayers, along with references to other worship resources already found in *The United Methodist Hymnal*. All of these items may be reprinted in worship bulletins for your congregation's use. You should choose one Greeting and one Opening Prayer for your congregation for each Sunday during Advent.

Unique in this section are resources to celebrate the Annunciation to Mary and the Visitation of Mary to Elizabeth (*UMBOW* 256-57). Traditionally, the Church has celebrated the Annunciation on March 25 and the Visitation on May 31. Because of the Protestant reluctance to venerate Mary, our previous books of worship left out these celebrations. Now, for the first time, our denomination includes these days and lessons, but encourages their observance during Advent. Both emphasize the significant role of women in the divine narrative.

BRIEF ADVENT SERVICES AND ORDERS

Hanging of the Greens (*UMBOW* 258) is an excellent service on one of the earlier days or evenings of Advent. This beautiful service of Scripture, song, and readings, out of a Germanic tradition, decorates the church and sanctuary with evergreen signs of the coming of Christ. To prepare for this service, you must prepare branches of cedar, garlands of pine and fir, wreaths of holly and ivy, and a Chrismon tree. Despite some caution about fire, the use of real (not artificial) evergreen is preferred. The service takes no more than twenty-five minutes.

A variety of brief orders of worship for Advent may be used in your congregation. The Blessing of the Chrismon Tree (*UMBOW* 260) and the Blessing of the Advent Wreath (*UMBOW* 261) both remind your congregation that every item in your worship encourages thanksgiving to God. The Lighting of the Advent Candles, which may be used progressively each week as more candles are lit, is an excellent act of worship to sing. Two new musical settings for the lighting of the candles in the book of worship (*UMBOW* 208-9) are wonderful ways for your choir, children, or whole congregation to participate. Regarding the appropriate colors of the Advent wreath candles, they may either be all purple or three purple and one rose (an ancient tradition to alleviate exclusive focus on purple/penance during Advent and to heighten the joy of the coming incarnation).

LESSONS AND CAROLS

An Advent Service of Lessons and Carols (*UMBOW* 263) is a new service in our book of worship. The service may anticipate your congregation's Christmas Eve Service of Lessons and Carols. It fulfills two needs during Advent: to hear readings from Scripture related to the coming of Christ, and to sing some favorite Advent/Christmas hymns. Your congregation may choose to use this service on any Sunday of Advent, although it may be better to put the service off until the Third or Fourth Sunday of Advent. Children, youth, and adults of all ages serve well as readers. If you ask people to read, be sure that you give them their readings well ahead of time and rehearse with them in the sanctuary before the service. Your choirs should rehearse and lead the congregational singing. An offering may be received between the Fifth and Sixth Lessons.

A worship bulletin is very important in this service. A bulletin allows the congregation to participate fully without being interrupted by numerous announcements. Especially encourage the congregation to follow along with the readings in their pew Bibles. If you encourage the congregation to do so, be sure to print the page number of the reading (not just the book, chapter, and verse) in the bulletin and read from the same translation.

LAS POSADAS

Las Posadas (Service of Shelter for the Holy Family; *UMBOW* 266) may become one of the most popular services in our new book of worship. Out of the Hispanic culture, this service recreates the Holy Family's journey into Bethlehem with a distinctive liberation tone. Children and youth will find this service to be exciting in many ways.

During the last days of Advent, Las Posadas is celebrated not in your church building(s), but in the homes of your congregation. As the service suggests, "on the appointed day, people meet at the corner near the home to be visited. In small communities this procession of pilgrims would take place by walking from one home to another, but in larger communities it could be a car caravan. Traditionally, there are persons carrying lighted candles and singing as they walk. In the lead may be Mary, seated on a donkey, with Joseph. Children, possibly dressed as shepherds and the magi, accompany the procession. Then, in procession, the people approach the unlit (darkened) house, and proceed with the following service."

Encourage the people, and especially the children, to dress in costumes for the service. When they arrive, provide each person with a bulletin with the text of the service. The service may then proceed in one of two ways. Traditionally, a whole neighborhood or parish participates in Las Posadas. Each night for eight nights, the procession of people knocks on the door of a first home, and then reads responsively the first half of the service (down through the James 2:14-17 reading) with the people inside the home. After James has been read, the people inside the home lock their door and turn off their lights, and the procession moves on to the next house. The rejection of the pilgrims occurs each time, until the procession moves to the final home, where the people inside switch on all the lights and welcome them inside. This model enables a whole community to remember the journey of the Holy Family, and thus reinforces the sense of rejection and the joy of acceptance.

Another, and more modest, service involves only one home on one evening during Advent. The company of pilgrims simply travels to one residence, where the complete service is celebrated. The liturgy itself takes only ten minutes. This simpler way of celebrating Las Posadas may be a good way to introduce the service to your congregation.

CHRISTMAS CAROLS OR ADVENT HYMNS?

The single most difficult problem in planning worship for Advent is the role of the Christmas carols and hymns. Your congregation may want to begin singing Christmas carols in church as soon as they are heard in the stores. Christmas carols, however, often celebrate the birth of Christ before Advent allows your congregation to prepare for his coming. Do not give up the struggle too early to preserve the integrity of Advent.

The best way to solve this dilemma is to provide other rich worship experiences and teach your congregation a new array of Advent hymns. *The United Methodist Book of Worship* provides a whole new set of services that will bless your congregation. Christmas carols are so beloved because of their association with the Christmas Eve Service of Lessons and Carols. These new Advent services can become just as meaningful. *The United Methodist Hymnal* provides twenty excellent Advent hymns and canticles, and the book of worship (*UMBOW* 239) provides an expanded list of hymns appropriate to Advent, as well as several new musical acts of worship (*UMBOW* 206-11). Once again you have a chance to teach Advent hymns to your congregation and use them throughout Advent.

ADVENT WORSHIP PLANNING WORKSHEET

_____   _____
Date   Sunday of Advent
Scriptures: Purple or Blue Liturgical Color
First _____   Will there be Communion?_____
Psalm _____   Great Thanksgiving: *UMBOW* 54
Second _____   Special Emphasis or Special Service:
Gospel _____   Hanging of the Greens,
                              Chrismon Tree, Advent Wreath,
                                               Advent Candles

Sermon Focus:

Hymns: *UMBOW* 239

_____
_____
_____
Anthems: _____
_____
Service/Communion Music: see *UMBOW* 239-40
_____
   musical acts of worship *UMBOW* 206-11
Instrumental Music: _____

_____
Greeting: *UMBOW* 240-48
Opening Prayer: *UMBOW* 249-54
Lay Liturgists/Readers:_____
Acolytes: _____
Other Participants: _____
Visuals: Advent wreath, evergreen wreaths, Chrismon tree,
   Jesse tree
Other Information: United Methodist Student Day

11. CHRISTMAS

Christmas is a season of praise and thanksgiving for the incarnation of God in Jesus Christ, which begins with Christmas Eve or Day and continues through the Day of Epiphany. The name Christmas comes from the season's first service, the Christ Mass. Epiphany comes from the Greek word epiphania, which means manifestation.

The United Methodist Book of Worship contains many acts of worship and services of worship for Christmas. In addition to the items found in the Christmas section of the book of worship (UMBOW 267-97), the book of worship also contains Prayers of Great Thanksgiving for Holy Communion for Christmas and New Year/Epiphany (UMBOW 56-59).

The Scripture readings for Christmas in the lectionary (UMBOW 228) exhibit a thematic unity each service and each day. The Old Testament, Psalm, and Epistle reading all revolve around the Gospel lesson. Always look first at the Gospel reading to set the tone or theme of the day.

Throughout Christmas, "use the colors of white and gold and materials of the finest texture for paraments, stoles, and banners. Signs of the season include continuing use of a Chrismon Tree, a nativity scene (including the magi on the Day of Epiphany), a Christmas star, angels, poinsettias, and roses. Gold, frankincense, myrrh, and three crowns are appropriate on the Day of Epiphany." In general, continue to display the Christmas visuals throughout Christmas to remind your congregation that Christmas is not just a day but a season.

The United Methodist Book of Worship includes the following worship resources for Christmas:

Acts of Worship for the Christmas Season
Blessing of a Nativity Scene
A Christmas Eve Service of Las Posadas
A Festival of Nine Lessons and Carols
Covenant Renewal Service

Acts of Worship for New Year's Eve/Day
Acts of Worship for the Epiphany of the Lord

ACTS OF WORSHIP FOR CHRISTMAS

The Acts of Worship for Christmas include hymns and canticles, short musical responses (which may be used as brief congregational responses throughout the services), greetings, and prayers, along with references to other worship resources already found in *The United Methodist Hymnal*. All of these items may be reprinted in bulletins for your congregation's worship. You should choose one Greeting and one Opening Prayer for your congregation for each Sunday and Special Day in Christmas.

Now is the time for your congregation to sing the Christmas carols and hymns they love so much. After using predominantly Advent hymns throughout December, sing the Christmas music for the next two weeks. You may decide to increase the number of hymns sung during worship. You may accomplish this either by deleting some other aspect of worship, such as an anthem or a collect, or simply choose to sing only a few stanzas of a wide variety of hymns. A hymn festival on Christmas Day or the First Sunday After Christmas Day is an excellent way to enable your people to sing the hymns they love so much.

As in Advent, a variety of brief orders of worship may be used in your congregation. The Blessing of a Nativity Scene (*UMBOW* 280) reminds your congregation of the Holy Family throughout Christmas, and it may become a model for use in homes. Bless the crèche on Christmas Eve or Christmas Day and be sure to leave it visible through the Day of Epiphany, and then on Epiphany add the wise men to the crèche.

LAS POSADAS

A Christmas Eve Service of Las Posadas (*UMBOW* 281) continues the service you began during Advent in the homes of your congregation. Even if you have not used Las Posadas on the eight nights before Christmas Eve, it is not too late to celebrate this service in your congregation. You may discover that for children and youth, a late afternoon/early evening service on Christmas Eve will be an exciting alternative service to the more formal Festival of Nine Lessons and Carols held later in the evening.

Encourage your people, and especially the children, to dress in biblical costumes for the service. Or your congregation may provide simple animal masks and costumes for children to put on when they arrive for worship. Be especially sure to have magi and their gifts among the company. When the people arrive, provide each person with a bulletin with the text of the service. Ideally, people will sing most of the service, using the texts and hymns indicated by the liturgy. At the conclusion of the service, which takes about twenty minutes, everyone moves to a fellowship hall or area for the breaking of the piñata and refreshments.

LESSONS AND CAROLS

A Festival of Nine Lessons and Carols, a classic service from Great Britain, is updated in our book of worship. The service now suggests only hymns from *The United Methodist Hymnal.* The festival responds to two needs on Christmas Eve: to hear readings from the Bible related to the coming of Christ, and to sing some favorite Christmas carols. In many communities, the service takes place later in the evening, even as late as 11:00 P.M., and involves an extensive use of candles. Instead of using the service on Christmas Eve, your congregation may choose to use this service on any Sunday during Christmas or even on Christmas Day. Children, youth, and adults of all ages may serve well as readers. If you ask people to read, be sure that you give them their readings well ahead of time and rehearse with them in the sanctuary before the service. Your choirs should rehearse and lead the congregational singing. An Offering may be received between the Fifth and Sixth Lessons.

A worship bulletin is very important in the Service of Lessons and Carols. A bulletin allows your congregation to participate fully without being interrupted by numerous announcements. Especially encourage the congregation to follow along with the readings in their pew Bibles. If you encourage your congregation to follow the readings in pew Bibles, be sure to print the page number of the reading (not just the book, chapter, and verse) and read from the same translation.

WORSHIP ON CHRISTMAS DAY

Although it is not specified by the book of worship, churches ought to offer worship to God on Christmas Day. Too often, our culture tells us that Christmas Day is just for families and football. This cultural bias often blinds us to our responsibility to worship God on this second most holy day of the Christian year. It also prevents us from seeing the need on this day to care for people who do not have families or who cannot be with their families. An early morning, midday, or evening service may celebrate anew the incarnation of God in your midst.

The service on Christmas Day (as well as on Christmas Eve) may best be a brief service of Holy Communion, using the Prayer of Great Thanksgiving for Christmas (*UMBOW* 56), along with brief readings from Scripture and the singing of Christmas carols. Invite people to dress casually and encourage them, especially children, to share the blessings they received.

COVENANT RENEWAL SERVICE

The Covenant Renewal Service, a traditional Wesleyan service for New Year's Eve or Day, has been restored to a more original form in the book of worship. The services appearing in our previous books of worship had almost nothing in common with the liturgy proposed by John Wesley over two hundred and fifty years ago. The Covenant Renewal Service now found in our book restores Wesley's own service.

Introduce this service to your congregation with adequate preparation. The language is stark, the demands rigorous, and the consequences explicit. Prepare the congregation for this service through study sessions, sermons, Bible study, and prayer. Participants should see a copy of the service in advance and should be expected to keep a copy of the covenant throughout the new year. All should know before the service begins exactly what covenant they are about to make with God.

An alternative service for New Year's Eve or Day is The Baptismal Covenant Service IV: A Congregational Reaffirmation of the Baptismal Covenant, found in both the hymnal (*UMH* 50-53) and the book of worship (*UMBOW* 288-94). This service, focused on the baptismal waters, serves well was a renewal of a person's covenant with God.

CHRISTMAS WORSHIP PLANNING WORKSHEET

Date: _____
Christmas Eve/Day, First Sunday of
Christmas, New Year, Epiphany

White or Gold Liturgical Color

Scriptures:

First _____ Will there be Communion? _____

Psalm _____ Great Thanksgiving: UMBOW 54-57

Second _____ Special Emphasis or Special Service:

Gospel _____ nativity scene, New Year
Covenant Renewal Service

Sermon Focus:

Hymns: *UMBOW* 270

_____

_____

_____

Anthems: _____

_____

Service/Communion Music: *UMBOW* 270

_____

see musical acts of worship in *UMBOW* 210, 212, 213, 216

Instrumental Music: _____

_____

Greeting: *UMBOW* 271-75

Opening Prayer: *UMBOW* 276-78

Lay Liturgists/Readers:_____

Acolytes: _____

Other Participants: _____

Visuals: Chrismon tree, nativity scene, star, angels

Other Information:

12. SEASON AFTER THE EPIPHANY

> *The Season After the Epiphany is a season of* Ordinary Time *which includes between four and nine Sundays, depending on the date of Easter. It is* ordinary *in that it stands between the two great christological cycles of Advent/Christmas/Epiphany and Lent/Easter/Pentecost, and has no one central theme or thrust. The First Sunday focuses on the Baptism of Christ and the Last Sunday on the Transfiguration.*

The United Methodist Book of Worship contains a limited number of acts of worship and services of worship for the Season After the Epiphany. In addition to the items found in the Season After the Epiphany section (*UMBOW* 298-319), the book of worship also contains a Prayer of Great Thanksgiving for Holy Communion for Epiphany/Baptism of the Lord (*UMBOW* 58-59). Because this is Ordinary Time, resources from the General Acts of Worship (*UMBOW* 445-567) may also be used throughout this season.

The Scripture readings for the Sundays After the Epiphany in the lectionary (*UMBOW* 228-230) exhibit a thematic unity each Sunday. The Old Testament Psalm reading all revolve around the Gospel lesson of the day. The Epistle lessons are not related to the Gospel lessons. Rather, they are semi-continuous readings from a particular letter. Each Epistle lesson relates to the Epistle readings of the preceding and following weeks. Each year, the Gospel lessons come from the early chapters of Matthew, Mark, and Luke, and therefore describe the early ministry of Jesus. Always look first at the Gospel reading to set the tone or theme of the day.

Throughout the Season After the Epiphany, "use white paraments, stoles, and banners on the First Sunday (Baptism of the Lord) and the Last Sunday (Transfiguration Sunday), with green on the other Sundays. The use of contrasting colors will help accentuate these more neutral colors. Visuals may include a baptismal font, water jars for the miracle at Cana, and bright candles for the Transfiguration." Because this is Ordinary

Time, do not be too bound by the colors designated. Let the color of the day, as well as all the visuals, reflect the focus of the day.

The United Methodist Book of Worship includes the following worship resources for the Season After the Epiphany:

Acts of Worship for Baptism of the Lord
Acts of Worship for the Sunday After the Epiphany
Acts of Worship for Transfiguration Sunday

ACTS OF WORSHIP FOR THE SUNDAYS AFTER THE EPIPHANY

The Acts of Worship for the Sundays After the Epiphany include hymns and canticles, short musical responses (which may be used as brief congregational responses throughout the services), greetings, and prayers, along with references to other worship resources already found in *The United Methodist Hymnal*. All of these items may be reprinted in bulletins for your congregation's worship. You should choose one Greeting and one Opening Prayer for each Sunday After the Epiphany.

The one act of worship most unfamiliar to your congregation may be the Presentation of Jesus in the Temple. Traditionally observed on February 2, this day celebrates the time when Mary and Joseph took the baby Jesus to the Temple in Jerusalem for purification on the fortieth day after his birth. The book of worship provides Scripture lessons, hymns, and prayers for your congregation if you wish to observe this day.

Baptism of the Lord and Transfiguration Sunday are the two holy days during this season. In each, the book of worship recommends one Greeting and one Prayer, in addition to suggested hymns. They stand as brackets for the whole season, and the Scripture lessons for each suggest some specific visuals that your congregation may develop.

SEASON AFTER THE EPIPHANY WORSHIP
PLANNING WORKSHEET

Sunday After the Epiphany

Date _____   Day in the Christian Year

White or Green Liturgical Color

Scriptures:

First _____   Will there be Communion? _____

Psalm _____   Great Thanksgiving: UMBOW 58

Second _____   Special Emphasis or Special Service:

Gospel _____   Baptism of the Lord, Transfiguration

Sermon Focus:

Hymns: *UMBOW* 298

_____

_____

_____

Anthems: _____

_____

Service/Communion Music: *UMBOW* 298, 302

_____

musical acts of worship *UMBOW* 210, 216

Instrumental Music: _____

_____

Greeting: *UMBOW* 303-307

Opening Prayer: *UMBOW* 308-316

Lay Liturgists/Readers:_____

Acolytes: _____

Other Participants: _____

Visuals: baptismal font, water jars, candles

Other Information: Martin Luther King, Jr., Day; Human Relations
Day; Boy Scout/Girl Scout Sunday

13. LENT

Lent is a season of forty days, not counting Sundays, which begins on Ash Wednesday and ends on Holy Saturday. Lent comes from the Anglo-Saxon word lencten *which means* spring. *The season is a preparation for celebration of Easter. Historically, Lent began as a period of fasting and preparation for baptism by converts, and then became a time for penance by all Christians. . . . Because Sundays are always* little Easters, *the penitential spirit of Lent should be tempered with joyful expectation of the resurrection.*

The United Methodist Book of Worship contains more acts of worship and services of worship for Lent than for any other season of the year. In addition to the items found in the Lent section (*UMBOW* 320-66), the book of worship also contains two Prayers of Great Thanksgiving for Holy Communion for Lent (*UMBOW* 60-63).

The Scripture readings for Lent in the lectionary (*UMBOW* 230-31) exhibit a thematic unity each Sunday. The Old Testament, Psalm, and Epistle readings all revolve around the Gospel lesson of the day. The First Sunday in Lent always describes Jesus' temptation by Satan, and the Sixth Sunday in Lent (Passion/Palm Sunday) is Christ's triumphal entry into Jerusalem and his subsequent passion and death. The readings for Lent are among the most unified and complex in the lectionary and need to be seen in their relationship to the lessons for each Sunday and to the whole season. Despite popular opinion, the lessons do not concentrate on mourning or the passion of Jesus. Rather, they prepare the people for Easter. Year A focuses on encounters between Jesus and a variety of his followers, a pattern of readings many people have found to be a primary description of how new Christians are brought into the Church. Year B concentrates on judgments by Jesus Christ. And Year C concentrates on Jesus' call to repentance. Always look first at the Gospel reading to set the tone or theme of the day; note how the lessons each week follow the readings from the preceding week and prepare your congregation for the next week's readings.

Throughout Lent, "somber colors such as purple or ash gray and rough textured cloth are most appropriate for paraments, stoles, and banners. Unbleached muslin cloth with red stitching is also appropriate. Remove all shiny objects from the worship area. Some may wish to omit flowers. Other visuals may include a large rough cross (possibly made from the trunk of the Chrismon tree), or a veil over the sanctuary cross." Especially in Lent, always let the Gospel reading of the day determine the visuals of the day.

The United Methodist Book of Worship includes the following worship resources for Lent:

A Service of Worship for Ash Wednesday
Acts of Worship for Lent

ASH WEDNESDAY

Ash Wednesday initiates Lent. The service is both penitential and anticipatory of Easter and centers on a most powerful sign-act: The Imposition of Ashes. The book of worship provides an extensive introduction to the service with many details about the structure of the ritual. A few additional comments may help prepare you and your congregation for this service.

■ The environment is crucial for this service. Dark and somber earthtone colors and rough, coarse cloth are appropriate for stoles and paraments. Drape the cross in a veil. Place ashes in a dark, earthenware bowl.

■ Make ashes several days in advance. It takes more time and material to create a small pile of ashes than you may expect. Do not put this preparation off until the last moment.

■ Provide a worship bulletin for your congregation. This will prevent you from interrupting the service with announcements. During the Gathering, describe to the congregation how the Imposition will take place, thus avoiding giving logistical details in the midst of the service. In the bulletin, especially if the congregation is not familiar with the Imposition of Ashes, make clear that people are free to choose whether to receive the Imposition of Ashes. Children and youth, as well as adults, are free to come forward for the Imposition.

■ The sermon should be brief, focusing directly on the invitation to your congregation to observe a holy Lent. The lectionary texts are the same every year and have already become familiar to many United Methodists.

The focus of the service is the Imposition of Ashes, rather than many words.

■ Rehearse ahead of time how you will impose ashes on the people. Be clear that you know how the people will come forward, where you will stand, how many leaders are needed to impose the ashes (anyone may impose ashes), and test how well the ashes you made work. You may discover that you need to add more ashes or a little water to your bowl. Don't forget a towel to clean your hand.

ACTS OF WORSHIP FOR LENT

The Acts of Worship for Lent include hymns and canticles, short musical responses (which may be used as brief congregational responses throughout the services), greetings, and prayers, along with references to other worship resources already found in *The United Methodist Hymnal*. All of these items may be reprinted in bulletins for your congregation's worship. You should choose one Greeting and one Opening Prayer for each Sunday in Lent.

LENT WORSHIP PLANNING WORKSHEET

                                     Ash Wednesday, Sunday in Lent

Date_____   Day in the Christian Year

                Purple or Gray Liturgical Color

Scriptures:

First _____   Will there be Communion? _____

Psalm _____   Great Thanksgiving: *UMBOW* 60-63

Second _____   Special Emphasis or Special Service:

Gospel _____   Ash Wednesday

Sermon Focus:

Hymns: *UMBOW* 324

_____

_____

_____

Anthems: _____

_____

Service/Communion Music: *UMBOW* 324

_____

musical acts of worship *UMBOW* 188, 201, 215, 217

Instrumental Music: _____

_____

Greeting: *UMBOW* 325-332

Opening Prayer: *UMBOW* 333-337

Lay Liturgists/Readers:_____

Acolytes: _____

Other Participants: _____

Visuals: rough cross, veil over sanctuary cross, perfume

Other Information: One Great Hour of Sharing

14. HOLY WEEK

> The Great Three Days—*sometimes called the* Triduum *or* Pasch—
> *from sunset on Holy Thursday through sunset on Easter Day are both the*
> *climax of Lent (and of the whole Christian year) and a bridge into the Easter*
> *Season. These days proclaim the paschal mystery of Jesus Christ's passion,*
> *death, and resurrection. During these days, the community journeys with*
> *Jesus from the Upper Room, to the cross, to the tomb, and to the garden.*
> *They should be seen as a great unified service beginning with a service of*
> *Holy Communion on Holy Thursday and concluding with the services of*
> *Easter Day. These services may be connected with a prayer vigil lasting from*
> *Holy Thursday evening (or Good Friday) until the first service of Easter,*
> *and may be accompanied by fasting.*

Although the resources for Holy Week are divided by the book of worship into the two seasons of Lent and Easter, it is exceedingly valuable to consider Holy Week as a whole. In addition to the items found in the Lent and Easter Season, the book of worship also contains several Prayers of Great Thanksgiving for Holy Communion for these days (*UMBOW* 62-67).

The Scripture readings in the lectionary (*UMBOW* 230-32) exhibit a thematic unity each day during Holy Week. The Old Testament, Psalm, and Epistle readings all revolve around the Gospel lesson of the day. Passion/Palm Sunday (the Sixth Sunday in Lent) retells Christ's triumphal entry into Jerusalem and his subsequent passion and death. The weekdays of Holy Week, the same every year, intensify Jesus' travail in Jerusalem during his final days. And then at the Vigil, your congregation hears again the whole of the divine narrative from creation to the triumph of Christ. The lectionary readings for Holy Week are the most unified and complex in the Christian year and need to be seen in their relationship to the other lessons each day and to the whole of Holy Week. Always look first at the Gospel reading to set the tone or theme of each service.

Throughout Holy Week, in addition to the visuals you already have used in Lent (especially a large wooden cross and/or a a veil over your sanctuary cross), use "red paraments, stoles, and banners and such symbols as perfume, coins, whip, crown of thorns, torn garment, nails, spear, sponge, or broken reed. On Good Friday and Holy Saturday the church may be stripped bare of visuals."

The United Methodist Book of Worship includes the following resources for Holy Week:

A Service of Worship for Passion/Palm Sunday
Acts of Worship for Holy Week
A Service of Worship for Holy Thursday Evening
A Service of Tenebrae
A Service for Good Friday
Acts of Worship for Good Friday and Holy Saturday
Easter Vigil, or the First Service of Easter

In general, all of these services and acts of worship demand great attention to the environment of worship and to the reading and hearing of the Word of God.

Passion / Palm Sunday

Passion/Palm Sunday is among the most dramatic of all orders of worship, as it encompasses both the joy of Jesus' triumphal entry into Jerusalem and his rejection and crucifixion. In earlier United Methodist traditions, these two foci—celebration and rejection—were celebrated on two separate Sundays: Passion Sunday observed on the Fifth Sunday in Lent, and Palm Sunday observed on the Sixth Sunday in Lent. This earlier pattern created at least two difficulties: (1) the Sundays were out of chronological sequence, and (2) the joy of Palm Sunday made it difficult to hear the pain and hurt of Holy Week. In response, since 1983 United Methodist and ecumenical resources have encouraged merging together the passion and palm observances.

The title of the day denotes the primary emphasis of the service of worship: the passion is more important in salvation history than is the palm celebration. The readings for the day reflect this emphasis, and the majority of English-speaking churches name the day Passion/Palm Sunday. The name of the day, however, has created some confusion. The name itself is not in chronological sequence, the palms do come before the passion, and many people grew up naming the Last Sunday in Lent as

Palm Sunday. You may choose to name the day Palm/Passion Sunday. But whatever you name the day, do keep both foci.

One primary way to keep the dual focus is by your use of visuals. Make sure that palm branches and a large wooden cross are front and center. Secondary symbols may include coins, a whip, or nails. Read carefully the passion narrative for the day; it will tell you what signs will reinforce the reading of the day.

■ As you plan this service, there are two major actions—Entrance with the Palms and the Proclamation of the Passion Story—that demanded the most attention. The Entrance with the Palms is the first major movement of the service. The more joyful you make this part of the service, the more powerful the reading of the passion narrative will become. Several weeks before the service, appoint someone to find or purchase palm fronds or the leaves of other trees or shrubs. Have them clean, dry, and in sufficient quantity for the whole congregation. Rehearse your children during Sunday school and ask them to lead the congregation in its procession. Plan carefully where the procession will begin, what path it will follow, and whether you will collect the leaves or let the people keep them to remember the day. Finally, as your congregation processes, make sure that the musicians continue playing the hymns chosen or other music until everyone is in place.

■ The Proclamation of the Passion Story is the second major activity in the service. The book of worship suggests three basic ways (along with variations) to read the passion narratives from Matthew, Mark, or Luke. The full passion narrative from each Gospel (approximately two chapters from each book) will take approximately fifteen to twenty minutes. Choose your readers carefully, provide them with their text in advance, rehearse together, and then let the Holy Spirit guide the reading. When done well, this service will enable your congregation to recapture the full drama of Holy Week and set the stage for significant spiritual encounters throughout the next seven days.

ACTS OF WORSHIP FOR HOLY WEEK

Midday services of worship may characterize the worship in your congregation during Holy Week. To assist you in this ministry, the book of worship includes three Greetings (any one of which may be used on any day of Holy Week) and four prayers for Monday through Thursday of Holy Week.

On Monday, Tuesday, and Wednesday, you may have a simple midday or evening meal (often a vegetarian meal with profits going to feed the poor), preceded or followed by a Service of the Word or Daily

Praise and Prayer. If you observe a Service of the Word, keep it short and focused on the readings from the lectionary (*UMBOW* 231). If you use one of the Orders of Daily Praise and Prayer (*UMBOW* 568-80), substitute the collect of the day for the opening prayer, or use the collect of the day during the Prayers of the People, use the psalm for the day of Holy Week instead of the psalm for the Order, and read just one of the three lessons (ideally the lesson from John).

HOLY THURSDAY EVENING

Two generations ago, the majority of United Methodist congregations did not observe worship on the Thursday of Holy Week. Today, it is a given part of the worship life in almost every congregation.

Like Passion/Palm Sunday, the name may create some confusion for your congregation. The traditional name, Maundy Thursday, does not refer to a service of grief or mourning, but a service that includes footwashing. Holy Thursday describes a service with or without footwashing. Your congregation may call the day Maundy Thursday, however, and not include footwashing.

Visuals and the environment are again very important. Whether or not you include footwashing, a basin and towel should be visible to the congregation. As throughout Lent, a whip, a broken reed, or coins may be placed before the congregation. Read again the Scripture lesson for the day and let it tell you what signs will enhance this service of worship.

The full service in the book of worship has six distinctive actions. As the book of worship specifies, the essential three elements of the service are Confession and Pardon, Proclamation and Response, and Holy Communion. Most services will include these three elements.

The other three actions—Footwashing, Stripping of the Church, and Tenebrae—greatly enhance the service and can easily and powerfully be introduced to the congregation. Footwashing, described in detail in the introduction to the service in the book of worship, is the most difficult element to add. Spend some time in advance, in Sunday school classes or Bible study classes, talking about the actions and describing how you will wash one another's feet. Especially alert people that pantyhose present certain difficulties for women participating in the service. When the time comes for the footwashing, be clear that people may choose whether to participate. Even persons who watch a footwashing will be strengthened.

Stripping of the Church, also described in detail in the introduction to the service in the book of worship, takes about three minutes and reshapes the entire worship experience. As people watch in silence, the worship space is transformed from the familiar to the stark. Persons are then prepared to hear the passion narrative from John (in the Service of Tenebrae) and will rejoice when the worship space is transformed again at the Easter Vigil.

If you decide to worship on Good Friday, especially with a Service of Tenebrae, stop the Holy Thursday service after the Stripping of the Church and send the people out in silence. By omitting a Dismissal with Blessing, you demonstrate the essential unity of all the services of worship during the Great Three Days.

A SERVICE OF TENEBRAE

A Service of Tenebrae may serve either as the last action of worship on Holy Thursday or as a separate service on Good Friday. Either way, it reinforces the passion narrative read on Passion/Palm Sunday and prepares the way into Holy Saturday and the joy of the Easter Vigil.

As with many other services, the two most important elements in this service are the environment and the reading of The Passion of our Lord. The environment, following the Stripping of the Church, should be bare and austere. The primary signs are fourteen candles, a central Christ candle (a large, freestanding white candle), and possibly a large, rough, wooden cross.

The reading of John's narrative will take approximately twenty minutes. It is better for the congregation not to follow along with the reader, but to close their eyes or focus on the candles and listen to the Word. You will enhance the service if you do not provide a worship bulletin, but simply announce the opening and closing hymns. As always, prepare the readers and rehearse together, especially in relationship to the extinguishing of the candles.

GOOD FRIDAY

The Service for Good Friday is stark and striking, focusing on meditations and prayers at the cross. The cross itself, ideally a large, rough, wooden cross, stands at the front and center of your congregation. All attention is guided toward that cross. Because of the Stripping of the Church on Holy Thursday, all other visuals from the sanctuary are gone.

Having secured a cross, prepare for this service in two more ways. First, rehearse well the reading of John's passion narrative. Allow the readers to practice together. Or even better, have the choir sing one of the choral settings of the passion. Second, rehearse well the reading of The Reproaches. Each of these ten complaints by Jesus about his

Church are powerful and strike deeply. Allow Christ to speak through the reader.

ACTS OF WORSHIP FOR GOOD FRIDAY AND HOLY SATURDAY

There are three brief acts of worship for Holy Week in the book of worship. Though brief, all of them point toward elaborate and significant services that you may celebrate in your congregation. The book of worship suggests that your congregation observe a prayer vigil leading to the Easter Vigil; these acts of worship may serve as a starting point for that vigil in your congregation.

The Seven Last Words lists the seven last phrases spoken by Jesus from the cross. On Good Friday, from noon to 3:00 P.M. (or in just one hour from 2:00 to 3:00 P.M.) these seven lessons are read. Following each reading, you may pray aloud, pray in silence, sing a hymn, mime the Scripture, or respond to the text in a variety of other ways. Our Church does not now have a full service for these words of Jesus, but your congregation may develop its own service. If you have individuals who are creative in music, drama, dance, or the visual arts, this is the time to put them to work.

The Way of the Cross is very similar to the Seven Last Words. This text includes fourteen biblical moments from Christ's journey from Gethsemane to the tomb. (The biblical narrative includes more than fourteen moments, but the tradition encourages the use of only fourteen. You may wish to expand or limit the number in your congregation.) Like the Seven Last Words, the reading of these texts encourages your congregation to contemplate Christ's journey, and it enables them to participate in that passion. Again, our denomination does not have a full service for the Way of the Cross, but your congregation may create its own worship service. Use the creative individuals in your congregation to create music, drama, dance, and visuals for your whole congregation.

Finally, the book of worship includes one collect for Holy Saturday. Although few congregations worship on this holy day, you may wish to observe this day of Christ's death with a brief prayer service using the Orders of Daily Praise and Prayer with this collect. If you choose to observe this day, remember that the worship space should be bare and the use of a candle or lamp would not be appropriate.

EASTER VIGIL, OR THE FIRST SERVICE OF EASTER

During the Great Three Days, from sunset Holy Thursday to sunset Easter Day, we celebrate the saving events of Jesus Christ's suffering, death, and resurrection. In the development of Christian worship, each event came to be remembered on a separate day. In the earliest centuries, however, these events were celebrated as a unity in an extraordinary single liturgy that began Saturday night and continued until the dawn of Easter Day. This was known as the great Paschal (Easter) Vigil. Preceded by a fast day, it was the most holy and joyful night of the entire Christian year, for it proclaimed and celebrated the whole of salvation history and Christ's saving work. It is the most appropriate time for baptisms, in which those baptized symbolically die and rise with Christ (Romans 6:3-11). It has also come to be seen as a most appropriate time for congregational reaffirmation of the Baptismal Covenant.

"The Easter Vigil is the First Service of Easter. The service which follows [in *UMBOW*] is an adaptation of the ancient Paschal Vigil service and consists of four parts: (1) The Service of Light, (2) The Service of the Word, (3) The Service of the Baptismal Covenant, and (4) The Service of the Table. The length of the service may suggest that the sermon be brief. Thus we celebrate God's saving work in Christ through the symbols of light, word, water, and the heavenly banquet."

The visual environment is crucial for the Easter Vigil. Setting the stage for Easter, "use the colors of white and gold and materials of the finest texture for paraments, stoles, and banners. . . . A focus on the baptismal font is appropriate. . . . A large, freestanding white candle called a *paschal candle* may be used. . . . Flowers of all colors are appropriate." Let the environment tell your congregation that Christ is risen from the dead!

You may celebrate this service in one of several ways. Do not be intimidated by its complexity or length, but adapt it to your purposes and the needs of your congregation. "(1) It may be an Easter Eve service, comparable to a Christmas Eve service, reaching its climax after Midnight. This comes closest to the ancient pattern and is appropriately called the Easter Vigil. (2) It may be a predawn Easter service, like a modern Easter sunrise service, but beginning while it is still dark so as to experience the transition from darkness to light. In this case it may be called the First Service of Easter and may be followed by a festive breakfast. (3) Because the service is very long, it may be divided into two services: a predawn/sunrise Service of Light and Service of the Word, followed by a festive breakfast, followed by a Service of the Baptismal Covenant and Service of the Table. With the Easter Day service, there would be a sequence of three different services that together would make a unity. Persons could attend any or all of them."

To prepare adequately for the service, observe the following steps:

■ The Service of Light requires significant preparation. Have someone or some group responsible for the fire and candles. Rehearse ahead of time and be sure that everyone knows what to do and when. If this part of the service goes well, the whole service will go well.

■ The Service of the Word can be lengthy and tedious if the readers are not well rehearsed and prepared. Each text is highly dramatic and requires readers who are passionate about their reading. Alert the readers in advance and rehearse with them. Alternating male and female voices is very helpful.

■ The Sermon should be short or omitted altogether. Let the reading of the lessons serve as the Word of the day.

■ The Service of the Water again requires rehearsal, especially by the pastor. Know what to say to whom and when. Walk silently through the liturgy to be sure you know what to do.

■ The Service of the Table will be heightened with the singing of joyous Easter hymns. This is not the day to be solemn. Celebrate Holy Communion with the most joyful of all the Easter music.

Finally, you will struggle over what to put in your congregational worship bulletin and what to leave out. If you include everything from the book of worship, the service may take eight to ten pages. This will probably only confuse and prove burdensome to your congregation. Leave out what is read or said only by the leaders of worship (such as the Greeting and the prayers after each reading) and include only essential information (such as the Easter Proclamation and hymns).

HOLY WEEK WORSHIP PLANNING WORKSHEET

Date_____

Passion/Palm Sunday, of Holy Week
Holy Thursday, Good Friday,
Holy Saturday, Easter Vigil/Day
Day in the Christian Year

Purple, Gray, Red, White Liturgical Color

Scriptures:

First _____ Will there be Communion? _____

Psalm _____ Great Thanksgiving: *UMBOW* 64

Second _____ Special Emphasis or Special Service:

Gospel _____ passion narrative, Footwashing,
Tenebrae, Meditation at the Cross,
Seven Last Words, Way of the Cross,
Vigil (light, word, water, table)

Sermon Focus:

Hymns: *UMBOW* 324 and 377

_____

_____

_____

Anthems: _____

_____

Service/Communion Music: *UMBOW* 324 and 377

_____

musical acts of worship *UMBOW* 188, 201, 215

Instrumental Music: _____

_____

Greeting: *UMBOW* 343-345

Opening Prayer: *UMBOW* 346-349

Lay Liturgists/Readers:_____

Acolytes: _____

Other Participants: _____

Visuals: rough cross, veil over sanctuary cross, perfume, coins, whip, crown of thorns, thorn garment, nails, spear, sponge, broken reed, or all visual removed

Other Information:

15. EASTER

The Easter Season, also known as The Great Fifty Days, begins at sunset Easter Eve and continues through the Day of Pentecost. It is the most joyous and celebrative season of the Christian year. Its focus is on Christ's resurrection and ascension and on the givings of the Holy Spirit on the first Easter (John 20:22-23) and the Day of Pentecost (Acts 2). Lessons from The Acts of the Apostles replace readings from the Old Testament because the early Church, empowered by the Holy Spirit, is the best witness to the resurrection. The ancient Christian name for this festival is Pasch, derived from the Hebrew pesah ("deliverance" or "passover"), thus connecting the resurrection to the exodus. The origin of the English word Easter is disputed, but may come from the Anglo-Saxon spring goddess Eastre and her festival. Pentecost comes from the Greek pentekoste, which means Fiftieth. It refers to the Jewish Feast of Weeks, which Greek-speaking Jews called the Day of Pentecost (Acts 2:1). Early Christians also used the term Pentecost to refer to The Great Fifty Days as a season.

The United Methodist Book of Worship contains many acts of worship and services of worship for Easter. In addition to the items found in the Easter section (UMBOW 368-406), the book of worship also contains a Prayer of Great Thanksgiving for Holy Communion for Easter Day or Season and a Prayer of Great Thanksgiving for Holy Communion for Pentecost (UMBOW 66-69).

Throughout Easter, baptisms, confirmations, and congregational reaffirmations of the Baptismal Covenant are highly appropriate, especially at the First Service of Easter and on the Day of Pentecost. Thus Easter is the preeminent time of the year to focus on the second sacrament of our Church.

The Scripture readings for Easter in the lectionary (UMBOW 232-33) exhibit a thematic unity each Sunday. The Acts, Psalm, and Epistle readings revolve around the Gospel lesson of the day. Often the Acts readings parallel the Old Testament readings during Lent. The lectionary readings for Easter are among the most unified and complex and need to be seen in their relationship to the lessons for each Sunday and to the whole season. Always look first at the Gospel reading to set the tone or theme of the day, and note how the lessons follow the readings from the preceding week and prepare the congregation for the next week's readings.

Throughout Easter, "use the colors of white and gold and materials of the finest texture for paraments, stoles, and banners. On the Day of Pentecost use bright red. Bright red symbols may also be used on a white background earlier in the season. A focus on the baptismal font is appropriate throughout the season. A large, freestanding white candle called a *paschal candle* may be used at every service during this season and at baptisms and funerals during the rest of the year. Flowers of all colors are appropriate. Visuals for the Day of Pentecost may include red flowers, doves, flames of fire, a ship, or a rainbow."

The United Methodist Book of Worship includes the following worship resources for Easter:

Acts of Worship for the Easter Season
Acts of Worship for Ascension Day or Sunday
Acts of Worship for the Day of Pentecost

ACTS OF WORSHIP FOR EASTER

The Acts of Worship for Easter include hymns and canticles, short musical responses (which may be used as brief congregational responses throughout the services), greetings, and prayers, along with references to other worship resources already found in *The United Methodist Hymnal*. Note particularly the Intercessions for the Weeks of the Easter Season (*UMBOW* 399), which provides one collect for each of the weeks of Easter. All of these items may be reprinted in bulletins for your congregation's worship. You should choose one Greeting and one Opening Prayer for each Sunday in Easter.

The Acts of Worship for Ascension Day or Sunday may be used on either the fortieth day after Easter (a Thursday) or on the following Sunday. This is a day that some United Methodists are now observing for the first time, and it affords creative expression in the use of visuals.

The Acts of Worship for the Day of Pentecost help you to celebrate this high holy day in your congregation. This Last Sunday of Easter has become one of the most popular days of the year. Again, the color red and visuals—including a dove, a ship, signs of the gifts resident in your congregation, and flames of fire—all accentuate the day. In addition to the Greeting and Prayers provided, this day is ideal for baptisms, confirmations, and a congregational reaffirmation of the Baptismal Covenant.

One of the most confusing aspects of Pentecost for many congregations is that the Day of Pentecost does not begin a new season of the Christian year but completes the Easter Season. It is the climax of the spring holy days, not the beginning of the summer.

EASTER WORSHIP PLANNING WORKSHEET

Sunday of Easter, Pentecost
Day of the Christian Year

Date_____

· White or Gold (Red on Pentecost) Liturgical Color

Scriptures:

First _____ Will there be Communion? _____

Psalm _____ Great Thanksgiving: *UMBOW* 66-69

Second _____ Special Emphasis or Special Service:

Gospel _____ Signs of the Resurrection (*UMBOW* 400)

Ascension, Pentecost

Sermon Focus:

Hymns: list on *UMBOW* 377

_____

_____

_____

Anthems: _____

_____

Service/Communion Music: *UMBOW* 377

_____

see musical acts of worship *UMBOW* 377
Instrumental Music: _____

_____

Greeting: *UMBOW* 378-391
Opening Prayer: *UMBOW* 392-394
Lay Liturgists/Readers:_____
Acolytes: _____
Other Participants: _____
Visuals: baptismal font, paschal candle, flowers, and on Pentecost: dove, ship, flames of fire
Other Information: Native American Awareness Sunday, Heritage Sunday, Golden Cross Sunday, Festival of the Christian Home, Mother's Day

16. SEASON AFTER PENTECOST

The Season after Pentecost, also called Ordinary Time, *begins the day after Pentecost and ends the day before the First Sunday of Advent. It may include from 23 to 28 Sundays, depending on the date of Easter, but the first Sunday is always Trinity Sunday and the last Sunday is always The Sunday of the Reign of Christ or Christ the King. The season also includes All Saints and Thanksgiving.*

The season is ordinary in that it stands between the Easter and Christmas celebrations, and the Gospel lessons pick up a continuous reading through one of the synoptic Gospels that ended on the next to the last Sunday After the Epiphany. Although many have difficulty with the concept, the Sundays After the Epiphany and the Sundays After Pentecost are all part of the same season.

"United Methodists have the option of calling this season *Kingdomtide.*" The book of worship (409) has a description of the history of Kingdomtide. You may, therefore, choose to name the Sundays during this time of the year "The _____ Sunday After Pentecost" or "The _____ Sunday of Kingdomtide" or "The _____ Sunday of Ordinary Time." It is best not to change the naming of the season after you have made your decision.

The United Methodist Book of Worship contains only a few acts of worship and one service of worship for these Sundays after Pentecost. In addition to the items found in this section (*UMBOW* 409-21), the book of worship also contains Prayers of Great Thanksgiving for Holy Communion for the Season After Pentecost, World Communion Sunday, All Saints, and for Thanksgiving Day (*UMBOW* 70-79). Resources from the General Acts of Worship (*UMBOW* 445-567) may also be used throughout this season, as well as the prayers and resources for the ten Special Sundays and Other Special Days during this time.

The Scripture readings in the lectionary (*UMBOW* 233-37) do not have a thematic unity each Sunday. The Old Testament, Psalm, Epistle, and Gospel readings all are semi-continuous lessons taken from very different parts of the Bible. Thus the Epistle reading in any given week is most closely related to the Epistle reading of the preceding and following week, and not to the Old Testament or Gospel reading of the same day. The same is also true of the Old Testament and the Gospel lessons. Unlike every other season of the Christian year, do not always look first at the Gospel reading to set the tone or theme of the day. Any of the three lessons may set the focus of the day. It is imperative, therefore, that the other worship leaders in your congregation determine which lessons will be the focus for a week or a month or for the whole season.

Specifically, in Year A, the Gospel readings are all the continuing narrative of Jesus' life as found in Matthew 7–25. The Epistle readings come from Romans, Philippians, and 1 Thessalonians. The Romans texts are radically revised from previous lectionaries to demonstrate more clearly Paul's central beliefs. Finally, the Old Testament lessons are distinctively different from previous lectionaries. Year A centers on the Pentateuch (the first five books of the Bible) and especially the story of Moses. It moves from the tale of Noah, through Abraham, Isaac, Jacob, and Joseph, to Moses and Joshua, and finally the conquest of the promised land. In general, decide whether to follow the Gospel narrative, the Epistles, or the Old Testament in this season, and then stay with your choice for an extended period of time.

In Year B, the Gospel readings are from Mark and John. The Gospel of Mark is too short to last the full five to six months, and so it is supplemented with readings from John. The Epistle readings come from 2 Corinthians, Ephesians, James, and Hebrews. The readings from both James and Hebrews more accurately outline these books of the Bible than in previous lectionaries. The Old Testament lessons are again radically new. The lessons focus on the development of the monarchy in Israel, concentrating on the first three sovereigns; they then move to Wisdom material—particularly Esther, Job, and Proverbs—and then conclude with Ruth and Hannah, as preparation for Luke's Advent narratives in Year C. Again, decide whether to follow the Gospel narrative, the Epistles, or the Old Testament in this season, and then stay with your choice.

In Year C, the Gospel readings are from Luke 7–23. The Epistle readings come from Galatians, Colossians, Hebrews, Philemon, 1 and 2 Timothy, and 2 Thessalonians. Each of the Epistle readings attempts to be faithful to the central focus of each letter. The Old Testament lessons represent faithfully the whole of the prophetic tradition, with a special emphasis on Jeremiah. The readings move from Elijah to Elisha to the pre-exilic prophets, with major emphasis (nine weeks) on Jeremiah and his message, and finally to the post-exilic prophets. All of the Old Testament readings are now in chronological order. Once again, decide whether to follow the Gospel narrative, the Epistles, or the Old Testament.

"Paraments, stoles, and banners can show a variety of color, texture, and symbols during this half of the year. Regardless of what name is given to this season, its basic color is green, symbolizing growth in Christ. White is the customary color for Trinity Sunday, All Saints, and Reign of Christ/Christ the King Sunday. Red is appropriate for homecomings, anniversaries, evangelistic services, consecrations, and civil holidays. The Scripture readings or theme for a particular Sunday may suggest particular colors, textures, or symbols for the visuals used that day. A lesson on children, for example, might suggest using art by children."

Remember that color is an essential element of your worship. Like all the other visuals and signs in your worship environment, the color(s) used in any service of worship may either enhance or detract from the focus of the day. Colors may vary, and there are no absolute rules that must be followed in your congregation. The key characteristic is appropriateness. Does the color you have chosen support the mystery of worship and serve the movement of the service?

The United Methodist Book of Worship includes the following worship resources for the Season After Pentecost:

Acts of Worship for Trinity Sunday
Acts of Worship for All Saints Day or Sunday
Acts of Worship for Thanksgiving Day or Sunday
Acts of Worship for Reign of Christ/Christ the King Sunday

ACTS OF WORSHIP FOR THE SEASON AFTER PENTECOST

The Acts of Worship for the Season After Pentecost include hymns and canticles, short musical responses (which may be used as brief congregational responses throughout the services), greetings, and prayers, along with references to other worship resources already found in *The United Methodist Hymnal*. All of these items may be reprinted in bulletins for your congregation's worship. You should choose one Greeting and one Opening Prayer for each Sunday in Pentecost.

All of the holy days—Trinity Sunday, All Saints Day, Thanksgiving, and Christ the King—contain Suggested Hymns, a Greeting, and a Prayer.

SEASON AFTER PENTECOST
WORSHIP PLANNING WORKSHEET

Sunday After Pentecost

Date _____   Day in the Christian Year

Green, White, or Red Liturgical Color

Scriptures:

First _____ Will there be Communion? _____

Psalm _____ Great Thanksgiving: *UMBOW* 70

Second _____ Special Emphasis or Special Service:

Gospel _____ Trinity Sunday, All Saints Sunday,

Thanksgiving, Reign of Christ

Sermon Focus:

Hymns:

_____

_____

_____

Anthems: _____

_____

Service/Communion Music:_____

see musical acts of worship

Instrumental Music: _____

_____

Greeting: *UMBOW* 448-473

Opening Prayer: *UMBOW* 448-473

Lay Liturgists/Readers:_____

Acolytes: _____

Other Participants: _____

Visuals:

Other Information: Peace with Justice Sunday, Christian Education Sunday, Rural Life Sunday, World Communion Sunday, Laity Sunday, Memorial Day, Father's Day, Independence Day, Labor Day, Reformation Sunday

PART THREE:

LANDSCAPING

You have now laid the building blocks—setting the foundation stones; planning for worship, preaching, and music; celebrating Holy Communion, Baptism, Weddings, and Funerals; and focused on the Christian year. What more can you do in worship in your congregation? The answer is landscaping.

In every congregation, there are particular celebrations and moments that call for worship. These special days and services may occur throughout the Christian year depending on the needs of your congregation. They add beauty and value to your congregation's worship life.

Special Sundays help us observe denominational and cultural festivals. Orders of Daily Praise and Prayer punctuate each day with hymns, psalms, and prayers. The Occasional Services remind us that every occasion in the life of the congregation is a time to celebrate God's present and promise. Healing Services recall a central ministry of the church. And Services Relating to Congregations and Buildings remind us that God is present in everything we create.

Use all these acts of worship to accentuate the foundations you have laid in your congregation's worship life.

17. SPECIAL SUNDAYS

The Special Sundays of The United Methodist Church are illustrative of the nature and calling of the Church and are celebrated annually. These special Sundays approved by General Conference are the only Sundays of churchwide emphasis. Such special Sundays should never take precedence over the particular day in the Christian year. The special Sundays are placed on the calendar in the context of the Christian year, which is designed to make clear the calling of the church as the people of God. Several give persons the opportunity of contributing offerings to special programs. The "Special Sundays with Churchwide Offerings" are set by each General Conference, to do deeds expressive of our commitment, and remain constant for a quadrennium. Other "Special Sundays Without Offerings" and "Special Sundays" with Annual Conference offerings are also set by General Conference. Annual Conferences may also determine other Special Sundays with or without offerings. Throughout the life of this book, such days are likely to change, and persons need to plan with yearly program calendars from the denomination.

Throughout the year, you will be faced with a variety of special days. Resources for these special days sometimes compete with the resources for the Christian year. Some of these special days overwhelm the lectionary readings on particular Sundays. Especially for congregations that use the *Revised Common Lectionary*, there are conflicts such as when Pentecost falls on Mother's Day.

For each of these days, *The United Methodist Book of Worship* provides a brief introduction to the day; a greeting, litany, or prayer; and hymn suggestions. The appropriate agency, commission, or unit of The United Methodist Church's general agency responsible for promoting the day helped choose these resources. By using one such act of worship, your congregation may recognize the day, but not be diverted from the central focus of the day as set by the lectionary or the church year.

The new book of worship divides these days into The Special Sundays of The United Methodist Church and Other Special Days. The basic difference between the two sets of special days is that the first set consists of days officially designated by our denomination for observance, while the second set are recognized in our *Book of Discipline*, but are not mandated for use in every congregation.

Some of these days have been a part of our tradition for half a century, others for just a few years. Some are recognized on particular days; others have dates set by Annual Conferences. Again, the book of worship makes clear that these days, while mandated for observance, do not take precedence over the celebration of a particular day of the Christian year. These days are:

> Human Relations Day
> Martin Luther King, Jr., Birthday
> One Great Hour of Sharing
> Native-American Awareness Sunday
> Heritage Sunday
> Golden Cross Sunday
> Peace with Justice Sunday
> Christian Education Sunday
> Rural Life Sunday
> World Communion Sunday
> Laity Sunday
> United Methodist Student Day

In addition, there are "Special Days . . . commonly observed in many United Methodist congregations and recognized in *The Book of Discipline* but not given churchwide emphasis. While set in the context of the Christian year, such special days should never take precedence over the particular day in the Christian year." These days are:

> Martin Luther King, Jr., Day
> Boy Scout Sunday
> Girl Scout Sunday
> Festival of the Christian Homes
> Mother's Day
> Aldersgate Day or Sunday
> Memorial Day
> Father's Day
> Independence Day
> Labor Day
> Reformation Day or Sunday

Each community will have special observances, such as Earth Day or AIDS Awareness Sunday, that also need recognition. You are encouraged to resource these days with greetings, collects, litanies, and hymns. Thoughtful planners will be careful, however, that the Scripture itself sets the direction and focus of the day, rather than the latest denominational or secular cause.

18. ORDERS OF DAILY PRAISE AND PRAYER

From the earliest days of the church, Christian worshipers saw the rising of the sun and lighting of the evening lamps as symbolic of Christ's victory over death. Additional hours of the day were also designated as significant moments of celebrating Christ's presence in the world. The Orders of Daily Praise and Prayer are a distinctive new set of services for our denomination, now found in *The United Methodist Hymnal* and *The United Methodist Book of Worship*. Many United Methodists requested such models of corporate prayer, and already these orders are becoming a part of our life together. They enable United Methodists in your congregation to celebrate daily the life, death, and resurrection of Jesus Christ.

The United Methodist Hymnal includes two of these services, An Order for Morning Praise and Prayer and An Order for Evening Praise and Prayer. *The United Methodist Book of Worship* includes both of these services, with additional prayers and rubrics, and also contains An Order for Midday Praise and Prayer, An Order for Night Praise and Prayer, and A Midweek Service of Prayer and Testimony.

"Each order may be celebrated in your congregation at a variety of occasions in its life together." Daily prayer may begin in the already existing groups of persons in the congregation, such as United Methodist Women, Sunday school classes, or an administrative council. Rather than starting a prayer group for using these services, encourage people who already gather for the work of the church to use these orders. The vision is that every time any group in your congregation gathers that group of Christians will pray together. In many congregations, this might mean almost immediately that at least once every day some members of your congregation would be at prayer.

Remembering that the early Christians generally worshiped in homes rather than in church buildings, and to encourage their use, the orders are appropriate in any setting, including classroom, fellowship hall, garden, or home. The use of common places for worship indicates that praise and prayer fit into ordinary life rather than being limited or reserved for holy places. Rather than sitting in rows facing a leader, "the communal quality of prayer is emphasized when the people stand or sit in a circle or other arrangement facing one another." In other words, have people face one another and not look at the back of one anothers' heads.

The titles of these services describe their pattern: the praise of God and prayer for God's creation. This is an ancient and classic Christian pattern of worship that grounds prayer of thanksgiving, supplication, and petition on what God has already done in Jesus Christ. These orders are designed to be short devotional moments woven into the fabric of daily life, rather than full services of worship that might include a devotional address or sermon. The focus must be on the scriptural psalms and songs read and sung, and prayers of the people, rather than a leader's meditation. By focusing simply on praise and prayer, no one has the task of preparing a talk (which excludes many laity who would otherwise lead the service), and everyone participates more fully.

To facilitate the lay leadership of these services, each order recommends a basic repertoire of psalms, canticles, hymns, and prayers. Leaders of these services should be able to guide these orders from either the hymnal or the book of worship with minimal preparation. By using only the psalms, canticles, hymns, and prayers recommended, very quickly your community will know by heart a basic core of music and worship resources that will sustain the people over a long period of time.

To maintain the focus on praise and prayer, the orders indicate that the reading of Scripture lessons, other than the psalms and canticles, which are then followed by a period of silence, is optional. This option of Scripture and silence is indicated in An Order for Morning Praise and Prayer and An Order for Evening Praise and Prayer by a large bracket in the lefthand margin. This does not suggest that Scripture lessons other than psalms and canticles are bad, but clearly distinguishes between a Service of the Word and a Service of Praise and Prayer. The use of Scripture in these orders is not to teach biblical truths or to improve our knowledge of the Bible, but to praise God.

You, as a leader of these orders of prayer, have two primary responsibilities: choosing music and texts for singing, and leading in prayer. Music can be the most significant part of these orders. The openings, hymns, songs of praise, responses to prayers, and Lord's Prayer may all be sung; the more singing, the stronger the service. While some of the music can be led without accompaniment, such as the Call to Praise and Prayer and familiar hymns, other music will require the use of a song leader or an instrument such as a piano. *The United Methodist Hymnal* has hymns and canticles for these services. Do not be reluctant to try some new music to enrich the services.

You will also lead the community in prayer. The basic pattern of prayer found in each order is one possible and well-tested outline of a corporate prayer of intercession (prayer for particular needs). The prayer moves in concentric circles from the particular concerns of your gathered community ultimately to the saints who surround us all. You begin: "Together, let us pray for the people of this congregation." Individuals then respond, speaking the name and needs of persons in that particular gathering. After each prayer request is spoken, you respond to the people, "Lord, in your mercy," and the people respond to you, **"Hear our prayer."** And so the prayer continues for people who suffer, the local community, the world, the Church, and finally it offers all of these prayers in union with the saints (including saintly persons dead, alive, and yet to come). If you feel comfortable using them, the musical responses to the petitions are excellent alternatives to a spoken response by your people.

Be alert to two concerns as you lead prayer. First, it may take time for the people to learn to pray in the call-and-response pattern suggested. Many persons are either eager to petition God for help for themselves, for others, and for the world all at once at the first moment of silence, or else can be reluctant to speak at all. When you introduce this prayer to people for the first time, it is best to remind some persons to respond to the specific petitions named, and to encourage others to speak aloud. With gentle guidance, your community will quickly learn to use and prefer this method of prayer. Second, do not feel limited to pray only in the way indicated by these orders. Each community of faith has particular needs and concerns, and you should always be responsive to those needs first. For example, you may choose to include a specific petition for persons in the hospital or confined to their home. The longer your congregation uses these orders, the more it will develop its own prayer language.

A few specifics about each of the orders will enable you to lead each of them more effectively.

An Order for Morning Praise and Prayer

This service is found in both *The United Methodist Hymnal* and *The United Methodist Book of Worship*. The people may participate by using An Order for Morning Praise and Prayer (*UMH* 876), while you use the order in *UMBOW* 569. The service in the book of worship provides an additional Prayer of Thanksgiving and more suggestions for hymns and musical responses. As the leader, it will be easier for you to work from the book of worship because it provides more details on how to choose acts of worship and how to lead the service. Otherwise, there are no differences in the two orders for Morning Praise and Prayer, and there is no need to print a worship bulletin for the service. Whether or not the people follow the service found in the hymnal, the congregation will need hymnals to say or sing the psalms, canticles, and hymns.

This service is for use by groups at dawn or as they begin their day in prayer. A breakfast of United Methodist Men or a Monday morning staff meeting is an appropriate occasion for the use of this service.

Visually, the service is most effective when morning sunlight is visible. The rising of the sun itself has been for two thousand years symbolic of Christ's victory over death.

An Order for Midday Praise and Prayer

This service is found only in *The United Methodist Book of Worship* (572), and only the leaders need a copy. The people will need hymnals, however, to say or sing the psalms, canticles, and hymns. Because you may lead the service by announcement, there is no need to print a specific worship bulletin for the service.

This service is for use by groups in the middle of the day, possibly before a noon meal or following a morning meeting. The order provides a brief moment of praise in the midst of a busy day.

Like An Order for Morning Praise and Prayer, this service is most effective when sunlight is visible.

An Order for Evening Praise and Prayer

This service is found in both the *The United Methodist Hymnal* and *The United Methodist Book of Worship*. The people may participate by using An Order for Evening Praise and Prayer in *UMH* 878, while you use the order found in *UMBOW* 574. The service in the book of worship provides an optional Service of Incense, an additional Prayer of Thanksgiving, and more suggestions for hymns and musical responses. As the leader, it will be easier for you to work from the book of worship because it provides more details on how to choose acts of worship and how to lead the service. Otherwise, there are no differences in the two orders for Evening Praise and Prayer, and there is no need to print a worship bulletin for the service. Whether or not the people follow the service found in the hymnal, the congregation will need hymnals to say or sing the psalms, canticles, and hymns.

This service is for use by groups as they end their day in prayer, especially before or after an evening meeting. This service is best used when a group is finished with its work, but bedtime has not yet arrived.

The primary sign in this order is a large, unadorned candle or lamp lighted and lifted up in the midst of the congregation. This sign focuses attention on the light of Jesus Christ that pierces the darkness of sin and death.

Turn down the other lights in the room to increase the dramatic power of the light.

The Service of Incense, optional as indicated by brackets, will be new to many United Methodists. The simplest way to use incense is to purchase a stick of incense, light it at the beginning of the order, and then extinguish it at the end of the service. The value of incense is that it increases the awareness that God's Spirit is everywhere and reminds your community that its prayers rise to God in heaven. Because incense will be strange to some people, and make others nervous, alert the congregation before the service and describe to them what you will be doing.

AN ORDER FOR NIGHT PRAISE AND PRAYER

This service is found only in *The United Methodist Book of Worship* (577), and only the leader needs a copy. The people will need hymnals, however, to say or sing the psalms, canticles, and hymns. You may lead the service directly from the book of worship, and do not need to print a special worship bulletin to lead the order.

This service of serenity and silence is for use by groups immediately prior to sleep or when retiring at night as they end their day in prayer. A youth group on retreat or a mission work team on assignment is an ideal occasion for this order.

Uniquely among all these services of prayer, the people may remain seated for the entire service. The key to the effective use of the service is for the people to be relaxed and for the leader to speak at a slow, meditative pace, guiding the people in a quiet voice.

Like Evening Praise and Prayer, the primary sign in this order is a large, unadorned candle or lamp lighted and lifted up in the midst of the congregation. This sign focuses attention on the light of Jesus Christ, which pierces the darkness. Turn down the other lights in the room to increase the dramatic power of the light.

A MIDWEEK SERVICE OF PRAYER AND TESTIMONY

This service is found only in *The United Methodist Book of Worship* (579), and only the leader needs a copy. The service does not follow the basic model of praise and prayer, as do the other services in this section, but is based on a Wesleyan and North American style of worship. Such services once characterized Wesleyan congregations and engendered life in the Spirit among the people. A number of congregations still worship with this style of liturgy, but until now, such a service never had been printed in an official book of worship. One hope is that United Methodist congregations will rediscover and use such midweek services.

This may be used for an informal midweek prayer service or a Sunday evening worship experience in your congregation. It reflects a style of worship in which the Holy Spirit and your worshiping community set the pace and direction of the service. Your congregation may use this order every week or only occasionally. Pastors and musicians least familiar with this style of worship are most encouraged to use it.

Worship bulletins are especially unhelpful in this service, but the people will need hymnals to participate in the service.

In planning this service, you need three primary gifts:

■ **Provide strong musical leadership.** Your song leader or accompanist must be comfortable responding to and supporting requests from the congregation. You may wish to choose one or two songs or hymns in advance, but then relax and let your congregation suggest which music is to be sung. Many surprising and exciting experiences will occur when you let your people lead.

■ **Guide sensitively the testimonies of the people.** As with corporate prayer, some people need gentle guidance to be brief and direct in their testimony, while others need encouragement to speak aloud. The greatest danger of a time of testimony is to allow one person to dominate. When persons do offer their testimony, respond to them. Following a testimony, a person may need a hug, a prayer, an admonition, or a word of support. You as a leader must give voice to the congregation's response to a testimony.

■ **Yield to the flow of the service.** While some leaders need to be in tight control of worship, knowing what will happen when, such control is inappropriate in this order. This service demands that you be flexible and respond to the unexpected. And when you yield to the Spirit, God will be with you and everyone will be blessed.

This expanded set of services of Daily Praise and Prayer enable United Methodists to reclaim daily prayer as a means of grace essential to Christian life. For an explanation of the history behind these Orders of Daily Praise and Prayer, and further suggestions for their use, see the Additional Resource in *Your Ministry of Leading Services of Daily Praise and Prayer*.

19. OCCASIONAL SERVICES

In addition to the General Services of the Church, *The United Methodist Book of Worship* contains a rich variety of services, prayers, and acts of worship that you may use on a variety of occasions in the life of your congregation; thus they are named Occasional Services. Some, like the Consecration of an Organ, may be used only once in a generation; others, like The Presentation of Bibles to Children, may be celebrated annually; and still others, like The Farewell to Church Members, will be popular and used frequently. Some of these Occasional Services are complete services, such as The Love Feast, which you may celebrate on Sunday morning or at other times in the life of your congregation. Other liturgies, such as An Order for the Presentation of Bibles to Children, are brief liturgies that you may include in a regular Sunday morning worship service. In general, texts that begin with "A Service" are full worship celebrations, while texts that begin with "An Order" are brief texts, which you may add to a Sunday service. The following are the book of worship's Occasional Services:

The Love Feast
Resources for Use in a Homecoming Service
An Order of Thanksgiving for the Birth or Adoption of a Child
An Order for the Presentation of Bibles to Children
A Celebration of New Beginnings in Faith
An Order of Farewell to Church Members
An Order for Commitment to Christian Service
An Order for Commissioning to Short-term Christian Service
An Order for the Recognition of a Candidate
An Order Recognizing One Who Has Been Ordained,
    Consecrated, or Certified
An Order for the Celebration of an Appointment
An Order of Farewell to a Pastor
An Order for the Installation or Recognition of Leaders in the Church

An Order for the Installation or Recognition of Church School Workers
An Order for the Commissioning of Class Leaders
An Order for the Installation or Recognition of Persons
  in Music Ministries
A Service for the Blessing of Animals
A Service for the Blessing of a Home

The following commentary lifts up several of the new services that may well become the most popular of the Occasional Services.

THE LOVE FEAST

This service is found in *The United Methodist Book of Worship* (581).

Until the middle of the nineteenth century, Love Feasts were the most popular of all Methodist worship services. Many congregations celebrated Love Feasts more frequently than Holy Communion, and in many communities the Methodists were known by their holy meals together. By the time of the 1965 book of worship, however, the Love Feast was placed in a section of historical services, with little hope that the liturgy would be used. By placing the Love Feast first in the Occasional Services, *The United Methodist Book of Worship* reclaims this service and restores it to our common life together. Encourage your congregation to experience a Love Feast at least once a year.

Like other unfamiliar services from the new book of worship, the Love Feast needs care and attention as you introduce it to your congregation. Initially, prepare the congregation by distributing in advance the introduction (*UMBOW* 581). One of the longest introductions in the book of worship, it provides both historical and practical suggestions for the use of the Love Feast. The more your people know in advance about the service, the more comfortable they will be in participating in it.

A variety of occasions are appropriate for a Love Feast. A Charge Conference, "where persons may report on what God has been doing in their lives and on the hope and trust they place in God for the future," is an excellent occasion that may transform persons' perceptions about Charge Conferences. "The Love Feast is also an important part of the practice of Covenant Discipleship groups," especially when a pastor is unavailable to serve Holy Communion. "Christmas, New Year's Eve or Day, the week days of Holy Week, and the Day of Pentecost are also fitting occasions for a Love Feast. A Love Feast may also be held during a congregational supper. The Love Feast has often been held on occasions when the celebration of the Lord's Supper would be inappropriate—

where there is no one present authorized to administer the Sacrament, when persons of different denominations are present who do not feel free to take Communion together, when there is a desire for a service more informal and spontaneous than the Communion ritual, or at a full meal or some other setting to which it would be difficult to adapt the Lord's Supper."

Bulletins may be helpful for this service but are not necessary. If you do choose to print a bulletin, include only the major headings and the one or two prayers and hymns chosen in advance. The worship bulletin itself should indicate that the service will be flexible and open to the movement of the Holy Spirit.

"The Love Feast is most naturally held around a table or with persons seated in a circle; but it is possible to hold it with persons seated in rows. A church sanctuary, fellowship hall, or home are all appropriate locations." Choose a location where people may see and hear one another and not be worried if crumbs fall on the floor.

"One of the advantages of the Love Feast is that any Christian may conduct it." The pastor need not be in total control of the service. At best, the pastor or other leader will simply guide the flow of the service and encourage as many people as possible to participate. Especially be intentional to include your youth and children in the service.

"Testimonies and praise are the focal point in most Love Feasts. Testimonies may include personal witness to God's grace or accounts of what God has been doing in the lives of others." Leaders must guide sensitively the testimonies of the people. Like corporate prayer, some people need gentle guidance to be brief and direct in their testimony, while others need encouragement to speak aloud. The greatest danger of a time of testimony is allowing one person to dominate. If this happens, be firm, encourage the person to complete the statement, and quickly encourage others to speak. And when persons do offer their testimony, respond to them. Following a testimony, a person may need a hug, a prayer, an admonition, or a word of support. Leaders must give voice to your congregation's response to a testimony.

"Praise may take the form of hymns, songs, choruses, or spoken exclamations, and may vary from the relative formality of an opening and closing hymn to spontaneous calling out of requests and singing as the Spirit moves. Sometimes the leader guides those present, alternating spontaneous singing and sharing in free and familiar conversation for a song as the Spirit moves."

Obviously, the Love Feast requires strong musical leadership. A song leader or accompanist must be comfortable responding to and supporting requests from the congregation. If someone, however, requests a hymn you do not know, do not hesitate to say so and ask for an alternate hymn.

You may wish to choose one or two songs or hymns in advance, but then relax and let the congregation suggest which music is to be sung. Many surprising and exciting experiences will occur when you let the people lead.

"Prayer is vital to a Love Feast. A fixed form of prayer may be used, especially something like the Lords's Prayer or Be present at our table, Lord." Spontaneous prayer requests and prayers may come from the people." It is especially valuable to sing the opening prayer of the service. The book of worship provides two classic texts and suggests tunes for singing these texts. The first prayer, by John Cenick, has always been popular, although John Wesley himself found the text too simple. The second prayer, by Charles Wesley, was written especially for Love Feasts. Of historical note, the Methodists in Great Britain and the United States have always preferred Cenick's text to that of Charles Wesley.

"Scripture is also important. There may be Scripture readings, or persons may quote Scripture spontaneously as the Spirit moves. There may be a sermon, an exhortation, or an address; but it should be informal and consist of the leader's adding personal witness to what spontaneously comes from the congregation." The leader must be alert not to dominate the service but serve as an enabler of the liturgy. This is not the occasion for a lengthy discourse on love, but is the time for others to tell how God has been a part of their lives.

"Most Love Feasts include the sharing of food. It is customary not to use Communion bread, wine, or grape juice because to do so might confuse the Love Feast with the Lord's Supper. The bread may be a loaf of ordinary bread, crackers, rolls, or a sweet bread baked especially for this service. If a loaf of bread, it may be broken in two or more pieces and then passed from hand to hand as each person breaks off a piece. Crackers, rolls, or slices of bread may be passed in a basket." You may discover a local baker or bake shop that will make special love feast buns (three-inch-round buns). One Moravian Love Feast bun recipe is a basic bread recipe, which then includes mashed potatoes, orange rind and juice, and mace. The youth or children of your congregation would also enjoy making the buns for the service.

"The beverage has usually been water, but other beverages such as lemonade, tea, or coffee have been used. Early Methodists commonly passed a loving cup with two handles from person to person, but later the water was served in individual glasses. The food is served quietly without interrupting the service." The primary caution at this point is not to provide too many options for drinks. If you provide too many drink options, the service will appear more like a restaurant with people deciding between beverages than a worship service.

"The Love Feast may also be followed by a full meal, in which case persons or families may bring dishes of food for all to share. During the meal there may be informal conversation in Christian fellowship, or the leader may direct the conversation by suggesting matters of mutual concern, or there may be spontaneous witnessing and praise. If there is food left over, it may be taken as an expression of love to persons not present." One of the best ways to introduce the Love Feast to your congregation is to celebrate it at a family night or church dinner. On such occasions, the sharing may occur before, during, and after the meal.

Your congregation will benefit in many ways by frequent celebration of a Love Feast. Primarily, it allows individuals the opportunity to share their faith with other Christians in a non-threatening environment, and it affords the whole congregation insight into how God continues to work. After your congregation tries this service once, it will want to use it again.

An Order of Thanksgiving for the Birth or Adoption of a Child

This service is found in *The United Methodist Book of Worship* (585).

When a child is born or adopted, sponsors and other family members may wish to present with thanksgiving the child to the congregation. This order continues the Evangelical United Brethren tradition of a congregational service offering thanks and praise to God for the birth or adoption of a child by a family. The order also has precedents in *The Book of Common Prayer* and in work by the Worship Commission of the Consultation on Church Union.

Many situations may call for the use of this service. The service may be used in a hospital or home immediately following the birth or adoption of a child. If parents or sponsors wish to delay the baptism of an infant, this order is also appropriate. Another situation for its use is when a family is related to two congregations; the baptism may be held in one congregation and this order used in the other. If a newborn child is not expected to live and thus is baptized in a hospital, and then survives, this order can then be used in congregational worship. It can also be an immediate act of worship with a family who need further nurture before they can take the baptismal vows with integrity. Finally, it can mark the adoption of a child already baptized. This service may become a popular way of celebrating this major moment in the life of a family and congregation.

This order best follows the sermon as a Response to the Word. During the singing of a hymn or act of praise, "the pastor invites those presenting children to come forward." Your worship bulletin does not need to include anything other than the title of the service. All of the prayers and actions are led by the pastor, who needs only *The United Methodist Book of Worship* opened to the correct page.

The order suggests that the ritual begin with "informal and spontaneous acts of presentation and thanksgiving." This is the time for the family, friends, and congregation to rejoice in the arrival of a new family member. This is also an appropriate time to announce the name of the new family member.

After a Call to Thanksgiving, the pastor may offer at least one of the four prayers found in the book of worship. Quite often, you may use two of the prayers, such as the prayer For the Adoption of a Child and a prayer For the Family. Your congregation then responds with a hymn, and the family returns to their seats.

In most congregations, the birth or adoption of a child is a moment of high celebration. This order will allow the congregation to celebrate this moment with integrity and joy.

A CELEBRATION OF NEW BEGINNINGS IN FAITH

This service is found in *The United Methodist Book of Worship* (588).

The Uniting Church in Australia created the model for this service in its most recent worship book, *Uniting in Worship.* Your congregation may discover that this service meets a fundamental need of some persons to celebrate publicly a new relationship with God.

This service witnesses to the fact that the Holy Spirit is constantly working in the lives of God's people, awakening faith and calling them to make a new beginning in the Christian pilgrimage. While many persons at this time wish to reaffirm the Baptismal Covenant others may wish to use this service. While a reaffirmation of the Baptismal Covenant concentrates on the reappropriation of baptism and often includes the use of water (in which case you would use A Baptismal Covenant I, see *UMBOW* 86-94), this service focuses on the new experience of faith itself and includes a laying on of hands without water. The language of this service is also less formal and encourages a time of witness.

It may be used to meet particular situations such as the following:

1. When a person has recently come to faith in Christ and desires to celebrate the experience and witness to it before the congregation in a service before or after Baptism.

2. When a person has recently made a recommitment of life to Christ.

3. When a person intends to return to active involvement in the life of the congregation. This service is ideal for those times, as at a revival, when a person offers himself or herself to God, but is not yet ready for baptism. This order would be ideal at the conclusion of a revival or

preaching mission, during a midweek service, or during or at the end of a retreat of youth and adults.

There are two major moments in this service, both of which require your preparation. The first is the time of witness. At this moment, "the person may give a brief witness to an experience of Christ of a new beginning in faith, or the pastor or another person may outline briefly the experiences that have brought the person to make this witness." Leaders should guide sensitively the Witness of the individual. As in corporate prayer, some people need gentle guidance to be brief and direct in their testimony, while others need encouragement to speak aloud. Be alert, however, that some people will not wish to speak aloud, and at these times a spiritual friend has the responsibility and opportunity to describe how God has been at work. When you must witness for the candidate, prepare carefully, as it will be heard as a direct report on how God continues to act in the lives of people.

Following this witness, the heart of the service comes at the Prayer with the Laying on of Hands. At this time, "the congregation, family, and friends may be invited to come forward and gather around the person. The person kneels. The pastor and others lay hands on the person's head." The pastor then prays for the individual.

It is important at this time to include the people most supportive of the individual's new relationship with God. A spiritual friend, Sunday school teacher, spouse, or other may well have been the initiating agent through whom God has acted in this person's life. Encourage these people to say a prayer on behalf of the individual. Encourage as many others who wish to come and touch, hug, prayer, and express love for the person. You cannot overemphasize the power of touch and the community bonding that it will create. And when persons do offer their testimony, respond to them.

Your whole congregation may be transformed when you celebrate New Beginnings in Faith. God is continuing to act in the lives of women and men, youth, and children. When God does act and people are changed, rejoice together with this service.

AN ORDER OF FAREWELL TO CHURCH MEMBERS

This service is found in *The United Methodist Book of Worship* (590).

The United Methodist Men's national organization, through its Moving Member program, discovered a widespread need for a service to bid goodbye to members of a congregation who are moving to a new community. This service recognizes that it is as important to say farewell as it is to say welcome. The order is an excellent way to send forth members of your congregation.

Before using this order of worship, you will need to prepare in four ways:

■ Plan to describe briefly how the person or family has contributed to the life and ministry of your congregation. In the case of a family, be prepared to offer at least a sentence about every member of the family and not just the adults. Other members and friends in the congregation may join with you in this time of remembrance.

■ Determine whether your congregation wishes to offer a gift to the departing person or family. A church history, a quilt, a cookbook, a photograph of the church or congregation, or a photograph album may be cherished gifts.

■ Be sure you have a clear understanding about when you will use this service. If you use the service only for some persons or families, and not everyone who moves, it may create some hard feelings for those who have been ignored. Some people will move before the congregation is even aware of their change in location, but when you know that a person or family is moving, a brief service will always be appreciated.

■ Finally, use the Moving Member program to alert other United Methodist churches that a member is moving into their community. One toll-free phone call to 1-800-624-4130 will ensure that your member who is moving will be welcomed warmly and may find another church home quickly. This ministry is a visible sign of our connectional system.

AN ORDER OF FAREWELL TO A PASTOR

This service is found in *The United Methodist Book of Worship* (598). In June of each year, approximately 20 percent of all United Methodist pastors say farewell to local congregations. After a period of conversation, consultation, and prayer, the bishop moves a pastor from one appointment to another. In most cases, the departure of a pastor is a sad occasion for congregations, the church members, the pastor, and the pastor's family. The same is also true when any other staff member of the congregation moves. Relationships developed over time, through a variety of crises and celebrations, will be severed. This service in *The United Methodist Book of Worship* provides a brief order to begin your planning for the saying of goodbye.

It is best for a pastor and several members of the congregation to plan this service together, although primary leadership must be given by the Chair of the Pastor-Parish Relations Committee, lay delegate to Annual Conference, or other designated lay leaders in your congregation. Do not lay the burden of this service on your departing pastor. The more laypeople are involved in the planning and leading of this service the better, and the following helps are specifically for the laity who have responsibility for the worship.

Before using this order of worship, you will need to prepare in several ways.

■ Determine the time and place of the service. You may wish to use a brief ritual in the midst of the last Sunday morning worship of a pastor's stay. You may also choose to have such a service at a church lunch or supper on the last Sunday. In general, more people will be present during morning worship, but you will have more time for remembrance at a lunch or supper. You may also have both a brief ritual during worship and then a more joyful time of saying goodbye at a lunch or supper.

■ Plan to describe briefly how the pastor and the pastor's family have contributed to the life and ministry of your congregation. Be prepared to offer at least a sentence about every member of the pastor's family, especially the youth and children. Several persons in the congregation may join with you in this time of remembrance. Remember that your pastor probably has been involved in the life of your congregation from youth retreats to funerals to weddings to baptisms to counseling sessions to building programs and many other activities. Have persons briefly state their own memories in their own words.

■ Determine whether the congregation wishes to offer a gift to the departing pastor or family. A church history, a quilt, a cookbook, a photograph of the church or congregation, or a photograph album may be cherished gifts. Plan to present this gift at the end of the time of remembrance.

■ Do not feel limited by the ritual in the book of worship. The prayer included is an outline of the issues that need to be addressed in the service: mutual love, support, thanksgiving, forgiveness, and hope. The aspect most uncomfortable to many people will be the time of asking for and receiving forgiveness by both the pastor and the congregation. But it should not be ignored. You may discover that you wish to expand each of these elements and create your own unique service of farewell.

■ A stole is the most visible sign in the service, and one should be included to enable the pastoral leadership to pass from one pastor to the next. Ideally, you may purchase or create a stole that will be unique to your congregation. Red, as a sign of the Holy Spirit, may be the most appropriate color. Symbols on the stole may include a picture of the church, the cross and flame logo of our denomination, or a dove or other sign of the Holy Spirit. On the last Sunday, your pastor will wear the stole throughout the service, and then, following the Dismissal with Blessing, take off the stole and leave it in view of the congregation. The following Sunday, when the new pastor arrives, give the stole to him or her (see the following service for help with this service of welcoming). The stole will be a sign of continuity and trust between the two pastors and between the congregation and its new pastor. The stole may be used at special events throughout a pastor's stay with your congregation. At the conclusion of the new pastor's tenure, the stole again will be left for the successor.

Saying farewell to a pastor is difficult, and the use of this service will allow your congregation at worship to say the right words and do the right things that will sustain everyone during this time of transition.

AN ORDER FOR THE CELEBRATION OF AN APPOINTMENT

This service is found in *The United Methodist Book of Worship* (595). Each year, the bishops of The United Methodist Church appoint or reappoint pastors to local congregations. This is the most visible symbol of our connectional system. The appointment of a new pastor fundamentally alters the life of a congregation, every member therein, and the pastor and his or her family. This is also true when the bishop acknowledges the employment of diaconal ministers in a congregation, and other persons join the staff of your congregation. This order provides one way for your congregation and its ministers to witness to their new life together.

A variety of people may plan this service. Avoid the appearance of the new pastor welcoming himself or herself by not asking him or her to plan this service. It will be better that the Chair of the Pastor-Parish Relations Committee, lay delegate to Annual Conference, or other designated lay leaders in your congregation plan the service. The outgoing pastor may also be helpful in preparing for the service.

It is preferable not to reprint this whole service in a worship bulletin. To reprint the whole text would create a great deal of paper rustling during the service. Your congregation needs only the opening affirmation and closing prayer printed in the bulletin. By printing only the minimal text, your congregation will also focus on the actions of the service, such as the giving of the Bible, and not on their bulletin.

Because laypersons guide this order, it is essential that they plan and rehearse carefully for the service. They should practice in advance who will say what words, who will offer each gift, and in what sequence all of the above will happen. This service includes several optional actions and statements (depending on whether the service is for a newly appointed pastor, a returning pastor, a diaconal minister, a staff member, or any combination) among which the leaders will need to choose.

The service suggests the use of at least seven items when a pastor is first appointed to a congregation. Although you may not wish to use all of these items, each is significant and important. Try to secure all of these in advance:

A Bible, preferably the pulpit Bible

A pitcher of water, which may be placed next to the baptismal font

A *United Methodist Hymnal*, ideally a new copy with the pastor's name on the inside

A *United Methodist Book of Worship*, again a new copy with the pastor's name

A *United Methodist Book of Discipline*, again, new copy with name

A globe

A stole, owned by the congregation and left behind by the previous pastor. See the preceeding service for a description of the stole.

Lay leaders may present each of these items to the pastor near to the place where they will be used. Present the Bible near the pulpit, then move to the baptismal font to present the water; move to the choir or piano to present the hymnal, and so forth. The worship space itself will dictate how much movement you can employ.

In addition, the leaders may select other signs of the congregation to present to the pastor. These may include keys to the church building, a church directory, a map of the community, a word of welcome from local officials, baked goods, or artwork prepared by the children. Poundings (an occasion when each church family presents a pound of a variety of staple foods to the new parsonage family) was the traditional way to welcome a new family in the parsonage. Be creative and see how warmly your pastor may be welcomed. Some of these gifts may also be presented to your pastor during a church lunch or supper on the first days of appointment.

When a pastor or diaconal minister has been reappointed to a congregation, it is important to use this service (only the prayers, not the presentations) on the first Sunday after Annual Conference. Each appointment is set for one year, and the pastor and congregation should state anew their relationship.

Finally, a church lunch following the service can be a joyful time for the pastor and the pastor's family to greet the congregation. Plan now to make this first Sunday a day of high celebration in your congregation.

A Service for the Blessing of Animals

This service is found in *The United Methodist Book of Worship* (608).
The Blessing of Animals is a favorite service in *The United Methodist Book*

of Worship. The service recognizes the intimate relationship between human beings and the animal world, demonstrates a Christian concern for all of creation, and affirms the Church as a steward over the whole of God's created order. As our culture increases its awareness of environmental concerns, your congregation may become a leader of ecological issues when it blesses animals.

"The Blessing is best celebrated during daylight in the outdoors: in the church yard or in a park." While some indoor worship spaces can accommodate this service, most United Methodist congregations use this service outside the sanctuary. Because the service attracts persons beyond the boundaries of your congregation, a park may be best.

The service "may be celebrated at any time of the year, and especially in early spring, or on the Feast Day of St. Francis of Assisi, October 4." Always set a rain date and publicize the service. You may also wish to celebrate the service in conjunction with other churches or organizations (such as an animal humane society).

"Make allowances for the arrival of larger animals such as horses and other livestock." It will not be unusual for people to bring goats, hampsters, birds, or snakes. It is best that there be plenty of room for the animals.

The worship area "may contain a table on which the Bible or musical instruments may be placed. Music is best led by instruments that work well outdoors: trumpets, accordians, drums, and guitars. Worship bulletins are awkward and should be used only to provide the texts of hymns to be sung." Because people will be handling their animals, too much paper will only create confusion. Instead of printing words to hymns, a song leader may simply line out a hymn or song for the people to follow.

The Prayer of Blessing is the heart of this service. The leader, with hands outstretched, may bless all the animals at one time. This has the advantage of being brief. However, it is often preferred that the leaders touch each animal and offer a blessing to each one. Be cautious, nevertheless, when laying hands on some animals; some enjoy being touched more than others. If you lay hands on each animal, you will discover great joy and be much appreciated by the animals and their human friends.

While this service will appear odd to some United Methodists, it is an important witness "to God's and the Church's love, care, and concern for creation." And after you have celebrated the Blessing of Animals one year, it will become an exciting yearly event in your congregation.

20. HEALING SERVICES

For the first time in the history of The United Methodist Church, a new category of services is found in *The United Methodist Book of Worship:* Healing Services and Prayers. These services are not new to Christians. As the new book of worship was developed, United Methodists requested healing services more than any other set of resources for worship. They reflect much study and went through many revisions until they reached their final form. With a strong biblical basis, already these services have gained wide acceptance and have become the most used of the occasional services in our new book of worship. They enable United Methodists to remember, affirm, and appropriate Christ's healing power in their own lives.

The United Methodist Book of Worship includes the following services and prayers:

A Service of Healing I
A Service of Healing II
A Service of Hope After Loss of Pregnancy
Ministry with Persons Going Through Divorce
Ministry with Persons Suffering from Addiction or Substance Abuse
Ministry with Persons with AIDS
Ministry with Persons with Life-threatening Illness
Ministry with Persons in Coma or Unable to Communicate.

When introducing these services to your congregation, the worship will be empowered by effective teaching, sensitive pastoral and lay leadership, and thorough preparation for the services themselves.

■ Prepare your congregation to use these services of healing by reprinting the introduction (*UMBOW* 613). You may also wish to print in advance the complete service of healing that you will use. Most United Methodists have seen healing services on television or in the worship of other denominations. Many persons are skeptical of the power and unclear about the meaning of Christian healing. In the weeks before your first healing service, share the introduction and other preparatory material in your church newsletter and in worship bulletin inserts.

■ Lay a strong foundation by preaching and teaching about healing. In Sunday school classes, Bible study groups, and worship services on the days before you begin the healing services, provide the biblical foundations for healing. Using the Scripture lessons found on *UMBOW* 616, remind the people that "spiritual healing is God's work of offering persons balance, harmony, and wholeness of body, mind, spirit, and relationships through confession, forgiveness, and reconciliation. Through such healing, God works to bring about reconciliation between God and humanity, among individuals and communities, within each person, and between humanity and the rest of creation." Many barriers are broken when your congregation rediscovers that healing is a central ministry of the Church.

■ Perceptive and passionate pastoral and lay leadership is the third foundation. Pastors and lay leaders together may lead these services. Pastors and lay leaders who work together will undergird the gifts that each brings. In every congregation, there are individuals who are open and ready to assist in this ministry. Also the pastors and lay leaders together should be open to the healing power of God and be comfortable inviting others to be healed. Leaders should have the ability to listen to the needs of others, to respond compassionately, and to offer a healing presence. Finally, leaders should be willing to accept the healing power God offers to them and through them.

1. Choose a time and place most conducive to healing. *The United Methodist Book of Worship* recommends A Service of Healing I at some time other than that of the principal weekly congregational worship service. This allows the service to focus on healing and does not coerce members of the congregation not interested in this ministry. As you develop your congregation's healing ministry, you may decide that there will be a healing service at a set time each week or month. The best location for the service is an intimate worship space where persons can move freely and have a place to kneel. A chapel, classroom, church parlor, or a member's living room are all good places for this service.

2. Select one Scripture text and prepare a sermon. The book of worship provides many texts from throughout the Bible, but one passage should be sufficient. Many passages were given because these services will be popular, and over time all of the Scripture lessons will be used. The sermon should serve not as an exegesis of the Scripture texts, but primarily as an invitation to healing. The sermon should be short and direct, and leave adequate time for acts of healing.

3. Determine whether you will serve Holy Communion. A Service of Healing I provides the option for the Lord's Supper and a Prayer of Great Thanksgiving for Holy Communion at a service of healing. To your advantage, celebrating the holy meal rehearses clearly the divine narrative and allows everyone present to participate. To your disadvantage, it may take time and focus away from specific healing ministries. The book of worship provides the option for celebrating Holy Communion either before or after the laying on of hands.

4. Choose hymns for the service. *The United Methodist Hymnal,* anticipating these services in the book of worship, has several wonderful and powerful hymns of healing. Some of these, however, may not be familiar to your congregation. If you choose an unfamiliar hymn or musical response, teach it to the congregation before the service begins.

5. Prepare for the time of prayer. Create in your mind an image of the persons who may attend the service, and be ready to pray with them. People will come with a variety of needs, and they will need particular and personal prayers. The following prayers for healing are found in the hymnal:

457 "For the Sick"
458 "Dear Lord, for All in Pain" (may be spoken or sung)
459 "The Serenity Prayer"
460 "In Time of Illness"
461 "For Those Who Mourn"
466 "An Invitation to Christ"
481 "The Prayer of Saint Francis"

Also be familiar with the prayers in the book of worship (626-29) for persons going through divorce, persons suffering from addiction or substance abuse, persons with AIDS, and persons with life-threatening illness. Every congregation in our denomination has persons and families facing these four crises. You may discover that you need to create a service specifically for one group of persons and focus on their needs and the needs of those who surround them.

In general, you be prepared to pray with the people coming for healing without using either the hymnal or the book of worship. While you should know the prayers in the hymnal and the book of worship and use them as the basis of your own prayer, a specific and personal prayer, explicitly using the name of the person, is always better than a prayer prepared and written in advance.

6. Prepare for the sign-act of healing itself. Be clear about each step and rehearse what you will do. Determine whether you will use oil in the service. As the book of worship states: "Anointing the forehead with oil is a sign act invoking the healing love of God. The oil anoints beyond itself and those doing the anointing to the action of the Holy Spirit and the presence of the healing Christ, who is God's Anointed One. Olive oil is traditionally used in anointing but can become rancid. Sweet oil, which is olive oil with a preservative, is available in any pharmacy. Fragrant oils may be used, but care must be taken as some people are allergic to perfumes." For your first healing service, you may wish to omit the oil altogether and use only touch and prayer. It is better to ease your congregation into the service than to overwhelm them with too much that is new.

■ If you choose to use oil, Thanksgiving Over the Oil is an optional blessing provided in the service. Use the Thanksgiving Over the Oil if you are comfortable, but omit it if it overwhelms the central focus of the service.

■ Offer an open invitation for persons to come forward for healing. You may need to specify that persons may come for healing of spirit, mind, body, or relationships. Determine whether your healing team members will respond either individually or as a team of two or three people to the persons who come forward. The advantages of one-to-one conversation are privacy and that you may serve people more quickly. The advantage of team ministry is that more than one set of ears will hear clearly what is being said.

■ Listen to each person as he or she shares concerns and needs. Do not attempt to counsel a person at this time, but quietly attend to what is being said.

■ Anoint, with or without oil, using the thumb or forefinger, making the sign of the cross on the person's forehead. If you choose not to anoint the person with oil, at least hold the person's hand, touch his or her head or shoulder, or hug the person. "Biblical precedent combines with our natural desire to reach out to persons in need in prompting us to touch gently and lovingly those who ask for healing prayers. Such an act is a tangible expression of the presence of the healing Christ, working in and through those who minister in his name."

■ Offer a brief prayer or blessing for the individual with your hands still on the person. Using the name of the person, make the blessing or prayer as specific as possible in response to the needs and concerns expressed.

Finally, sensitive pastoral leadership demands that the healing team members write down immediately after the service what needs were identified, and then remain in contact with each person who comes for healing. While counseling is inappropriate during the service of healing itself, Christian conversation and counseling are often needed after the service. The ministry of your church should not end when persons leave the sanctuary.

A few specifics about each of the services will enable you to lead each of these orders more effectively.

A SERVICE OF HEALING I

"This is a congregational service centered on healing and is designed for use at some time other than that of the principal weekly congregational worship service." Appropriate times for such services are Sunday afternoon, Sunday evening, a midweek service, or even Saturday evening. You will discover that if you advertise the service, persons from other congregations and the community will join your congregation.

The service is most effective when persons have worship bulletins and are able to participate in the corporate prayers. You may be able to use the same bulletin each time you use this service if you list the basic structure of the service, include the primary prayers you will use, and then simply announce the hymns and Scripture lesson at each service. In addition to the worship bulletin, your congregation will need copies of *The United Methodist Hymnal*.

■ A variety of colors is appropriate for the stoles and paraments for healing services. You may choose purple if the service will focus on forgiveness, or white if the focus is on new life, or red if the service concentrates on the power of the Holy Spirit. If you choose to use oil in the anointing, make the vessel containing the oil central and visible to the whole congregation.

Sharing of Thanksgivings is also a part of this service for which you must be prepared. After the anointing and laying on of hands, persons may be led to give thanks for healing and other blessings. You will need to guide sensitively this sharing. Some people need gentle guidance to be brief and direct in their testimony, while others need encouragement to speak aloud. The greatest danger of a time of testimony is allowing one person to dominate. And when persons do offer their thanks, respond to them. Following a statement, a person may need a hug, a prayer, an admonition, or a word of support. You as leader should give voice to the congregation's response to a Sharing of Thanksgiving.

A SERVICE OF HEALING II

"This service may be used in private or in corporate worship. It may take place in a church, home, or hospital, or at a meeting of a prayer group." While this service may be used in corporate worship, it is best for private use in a home or hospital, and may be used at any time an individual person has a need to accept God's promise of healing. All of the resources found in A Service of Healing I may also be used.

The distinctive part of this service is the Confession and Pardon. The service encourages the person present to share any trouble or difficulty that hinders his or her relationship with God. This service, then, is quite similar to the Roman Catholic sacrament of Reconciliation.

The service recommends that if you include Holy Communion, you use A Service of Word and Table V (*UMBOW* 51), a brief and flexible service of Holy Communion that is specifically for persons who are sick or homebound.

A SERVICE OF HOPE AFTER LOSS OF PREGNANCY

By some estimates, as many as 20 percent of all women (at least 1 in 6) after conception experience a loss of pregnancy. Until our new book of worship, however, our denomination was silent on how to respond to this traumatic situation. A Service of Hope After Loss of Pregnancy has become an exceedingly therapeutic service of healing for many United Methodists. Karen Westerfield-Tucker, a United Methodist pastor and liturgical scholar who herself experienced a loss of pregnancy, wrote the service. This service acknowledges that many women and couples face this situation, and declares that the Church has a ministry at this time. Any of the scriptures and prayers may also be used by themselves with a woman, couple, or family in private.

■ This service may be held in a church, hospital, or home after an early (first or second trimester) loss of pregnancy, commonly named a miscarriage. If the loss of pregnancy occurs later in a pregnancy (second or third trimester), the acts of worship suggested in At a Service of Death and Resurrection for a Child (*UMBOW* 161-62) or in A Service of Death and Resurrection for a Stillborn Child (*UMBOW* 170-71) may be more appropriate.

The congregation for this service may be small or large. In a few situations, a woman alone or several people together have read the service aloud and found the liturgy healing. In some cases, it will be best that the participants include only the pastor and the woman or couple. This liturgy may then take place in the hospital, the home, or the pastor's study. At other times, an extended family may be present, and you should lead the service in the church or in a home. And still other situations encourage the whole congregation to participate. This will be true especially in smaller congregations when the loss has been most traumatic and is felt by everyone.

This service is also one of the more controversial ones included in *The United Methodist Book of Worship*. The controversy centers around whether our denomination should state in a prayer that a fetus lost before birth may properly be called a "child." The pastoral reality, however, is that some women and couples choose to name that which is lost their child, while others wish to focus instead on the woman and couple and their loss. The United Methodist Book of Worship Committee decided that when a woman or couple suffer a loss of pregnancy it is inappropriate for the pastor to debate when human life begins. The parent(s) must choose. The book of worship, therefore, includes three separate opening prayers: the first concentrates on the grief of the mother and family, the second acknowledges the loss of a child, and the third focuses on courage and hope. The context in each case will quickly identify which prayer is most appropriate.

Women and men throughout the connections urge us to recognize the hurt and need of women, couples, and families at this time and offer this service as a part of your community's ministry through worship. By having this resource available, you will be able to minister well to these people.

For more information about healing services, contact the Director of Prayer and Healing Ministries, The Upper Room, P.O. Box 189, Nashville, TN 37202-0189.

21. SERVICES RELATING TO CONGREGATIONS AND BUILDINGS

The United Methodist Book of Worship contains a basic set of services and orders of worship that you may use on a variety of occasions relating to your congregation and the buildings out of which your congregation ministers to the world. For most congregations, each of these services may be used only once in a generation. Many times, bishops and district superintendents are called upon to preside at such services. Because most congregations and worship leaders have little experience planning and leading such services, the book of worship provides a foundational repertoire for your use. *The United Methodist Book of Worship* includes the following services and prayers:

A Service for Organizing a New Congregation
A Service for the Breaking of Ground for a Church Building
A Service for the Laying of a Foundation Stone of a Church Building
A Service for the Consecration or Reconstruction of a Church Building
A Service for the Dedication of a Church Building Free of Debt
An Order for the Dedication of an Organ or Other Musical Instruments
An Order for the Dedication of Church Furnishings and Memorials
A Service for the Consecration of an Educational Building
An Order for the Leave-taking of a Church Building
An Order for Disbanding a Congregation

Some of these are complete services, such as Organizing a New Congregation, which you may celebrate on Sunday morning. Other rituals, such as An Order for the Dedication of a Church Building, are brief liturgies that you may include in a regular Sunday morning worship service. Texts that begin with "A Service" are full worship celebrations, while texts that begin with "An Order" are brief texts, which may be added to a Sunday service.

Each service provides the necessary information for its successful use. The following comments apply in general to all the services, and each will ensure that when you lead these services they will communicate powerfully God's presence.

1. Your congregation will appreciate a printed worship bulletin for each of these services. Because these services are many times once-in-a-generation services, many people will wish to have mementoes. Also, because the services take place away from the sanctuary and the hymnals therein, print a special worship bulletin including the necessary congregational prayers and hymns.

2. Plan carefully the visuals you will use in these services. Many persons will remember waving banners much longer than lengthy litanies. For example, in A Service for Organizing a New Congregation, a new banner with the name of your congregation will be an important symbol on this day and in the years to come. A wooden cross at the place where the Lord's table will be located is important in Breaking Ground for a Church Building. Create a special task force of artists in your congregation to plan specific signs and symbols of each service.

3. Rehearse and choreograph the service. Rehearsed and confident actions by the leaders will always put the congregation at ease and make for a successful service. Determine ahead of time who will turn the first shovelful of earth, who will lay in place the foundation stone, or where to stand as you dedicate the baptismal font. Know where the matches are for the burning of the mortgage. It is much more appropriate to rehearse and walk through the complete service in advance than to fumble through the liturgy.

4. Select Scripture lessons for each service. While the lessons are each appropriate for the services, you may also use them to stimulate our own choices for Scripture. You are not limited by the lessons printed. Likewise, the suggested hymns and musical acts of worship throughout should stimulate your own hymn selections. Such services are excellent times both to sing the traditional favorites of your congregation and to introduce new texts and tunes.

5. Almost every service includes the suggestion to celebrate Holy Communion. This is not an attempt to lengthen the services, but to remind your congregation that the saving power of God through Jesus Christ forms the Church universal. Especially in these services relating to congregations and buildings, there is no better time to celebrate Holy Communion.

While there is some tendency to use exclusively the professional staff of your congregation, and at times your district superintendent and bishop, you must involve the lay leadership in these services. Over time, it is the laity of your congregation who are responsible for the congregation and the buildings. Your congregation's lay leader, chair of the Administrative Board or Administrative Council, other adult leaders, as well as youth and children can and should participate in these services.

Each of these services is very important in the life of a congregation. Each witnesses to how a congregation has committed itself to a particular place and community. Let the liturgy proclaim with thanksgiving what both the congregation and God are and will be doing in that chosen space.

ADDITIONAL RESOURCES

Visit your Cokesbury bookstore or call toll free the Cokesbury Service Center, 1-800-672-1789; P.O. Box 801, Nashville, TN 37202. Or contact Discipleship Resources, 613-340-7284; P.O. Box 840, Nashville, TN 37202-0840. Both Cokesbury and Discipleship Resources provide comprehensive catalogs upon request.

The following is a list of basics that all United Methodist planners and leaders of worship should have:

The United Methodist Hymnal: Book of United Methodist Worship (UMPH, 1989). Our official hymnal and worship book.

The Worship Resources of The United Methodist Hymnal, edited by Hoyt Hickman (Abingdon, 1991). *The Hymns of The United Methodist Hymnal,* edited by Diana Sanchez (Abingdon, 1991). These books provide essential background information to assist pastors, musicians and other leaders of worship in using *The United Methodist Hymnal.*

The United Methodist Book of Worship (UMPH, 1992). Our official book of worship for planners and leaders of worship.

Guidelines for Worship Work Area: 1993-1996 (UMPH, 1992). Job description of chair of worship work area in the local congregation.

United Methodist Music and Worship Planner, David Bone and Mary Scifres (Abingdon). Published annually with lectionary readings in their entirety, suggested colors, hymn suggestions, anthem suggestions, instrumental suggestions, and worship planning sheets.

Revised Common Lectionary, by Consultation on Common Texts (Abingdon, 1992). The complete three-year cycle of readings, including all alternatives recognized by other traditions.

United Methodist Worship, by Hoyt L. Hickman (Cokesbury, 1991). An introduction to United Methodist worship for personal or group study.

Worship and Evangelism, by Andy Langford and Sally Overby Langford (Discipleship Resources, 1989). Relating worship and evangelism.

Workbook on Communion and Baptism, by Hoyt L. Hickman (Discipleship Resources, 1990). A basic study book on the sacraments for laypersons.

United Methodist Altars, by Hoyt L. Hickman (Abingdon, 1991). A manual for all who do the work of altar guilds and a resource for pastors and worship chairpersons.

Song Leading, by Dean B. McIntyre (Discipleship Resources, 1989). A guide for ways in which your congregation can be led to more wholehearted and effective singing.

God's Children in Worship (Discipleship Resources, 1988). A multi-media kit for children, parents, and congregations to encourage the full and active participation of children in worship.

Upper Room Catalog. A free catalog of prayer, worship, and devotional resources. The Upper Room, P.O. Box 189, Nashville, TN 37202-0189.

Forbid Them Not: Involving Children in Sunday Worship by Carolyn Brown, Years A, B, C. (Abingdon)

The following aids for the *Revised Common Lectionary* are now available from Abingdon Press and sold in Cokesbury Stores or other bookstores:

Preaching the Revised Common Lectionary, 4 vols. per years A, B, and C, by Marion Soards, Thomas Dozeman, and Kendall McCabe, 1992, 1993, 1994.

Living with the Lectionary, by Eugene Lowry, 1992.

The Lectionary Bible, complete readings based on the New Revised Standard Version, 1992.

Litanies and Other Prayers for the Revised Common Lectionary, Years A, B, C, by Everett Tilson and Phylis Cole, 1992, 1993, 1994.

Your Ministry of series is a set of booklets that tell how to do worship-related jobs in local churches. (Discipleship Resources)

Planning Worship Each Week, by Hoyt L. Hickman.

Nursing Home Worship, by Raymond J. Council.

Planning a Christian Wedding, by M. Lawrence Snow.

Ushering and Greeting, by Kenneth M. Johnson.

Reading Scripture Aloud, by Richard F. Ward.

Planning a Christian Funeral, by Andy Langford.

Listening to Sermons, by Houston Parks.

Being a Communion Steward, by Hoyt L. Hickman.

Leading Services of Daily Praise and Prayer, by Andy Langford.

Planning and Leading Hymn Festivals, by Diana Sanchez.

Singing in the Church Choir, by Roger Deschner.
Being an Acolyte, by Michael O'Donnell.
Designing the Worship Bulletin, by David A. Wiltse.
Singing the Psalms, by Dwight W. Vogel.
Praying in the Congregation, by Sara and Ed Webb-Phillips.
Drama in the Local Congregation, by Lynda Ryan.

WORSHIP ORGANIZATIONS

Section of Worship, General Board of Discipleship, includes our denomination's professional staff in the areas of liturgy, music, and preaching. Contact the Section staff regarding workshops and further information and assistance regarding any area of worship. Address: P.O. Box 840, Nashville, TN 37202-0840. Phone 615-340-7070.

The Fellowship of United Methodists in Worship, Music and Other Arts, a membership organization, offers national, regional, and conference-wide training events in all the worship arts, as well as their journal *Worship Arts.* Address: P.O. Box 24787, Nashville, TN 37202.

The Order of Saint Luke is a United Methodist religious order, dedicated to sacramental and liturgical scholarship, education, and practice, and produces the worship journals *Sacramental Life* and *Doxology.* Address: P.O. Box 62, Corning, NY 14830.

INDEX TO *THE UNITED METHODIST* *BOOK OF WORSHIP*

[Note: Some elements in the major services remain constant, and after the first entry, only those that provide specific new text or rubrics are indexed separately. Items designated as 'orders' for brief services include appropriate hymns, prayers, and Scripture that are not indexed separately.]

THE UNITED METHODIST BOOK OF WORSHIP SCRIPTURE INDEX

(Note: The Lectionary is not indexed.)